THE SERPENT IN THE GARDEN

A LIFE UNRAVELLED

Dr. Vaidyanathan S. M.

First Edition: January 2026
Printed in India

Printed at: Thomson Press, New Delhi

Typeset in Adobe Garamond Pro

ISBN: 978-93-6070-227-4

Cover Design: Megh Haria

STORYMIRROR
Stories that reflect you

Publisher: StoryMirror Infotech Pvt. Ltd.
Unit No-F/705, 7th Floor, Kailas Corporate Lounge,
Veer Savarkar Road, Vikhroli Park Site,
Vikhroli West, Mumbai-400079,
Maharashtra, India.

Web: storymirror.com
Facebook: @storymirror
Twitter: @story_mirror
Instagram: @storymirror
Email: marketing@storymirror.com

DISCLAIMER

The names, identifying characteristics, and specific details of certain individuals and situations may have been altered or omitted to protect privacy and for narrative purposes. Any resemblance to actual persons, living or dead, or actual events, is largely coincidental, except where intentionally depicted as part of the author's personal journey.

The insights, psychological observations, and warnings contained within this book are derived solely from the author's personal experiences and reflections. They are not intended to serve as professional legal, financial, psychological, or medical advice. Readers should not rely on the information provided herein as a substitute for professional consultation.

This book discusses sensitive topics including but not limited to betrayal, financial distress, emotional struggles, and personal disillusionment. Reader discretion is advised. The author and publisher are not liable for any direct, indirect, incidental, consequential, or punitive damages arising from the use or interpretation of the content within this book.

By reading this book, you acknowledge and agree that the author and publisher are not responsible for any adverse outcomes resulting from the

Application of the information or perspectives shared herein.

Important Disclaimer and Acknowledgement

The wisdom and life lessons shared herein are largely drawn from the profound works of numerous authors and books that have significantly influenced my personal journey. I extend my deepest gratitude and heartfelt appreciation to these remarkable individuals. Their insights have served as invaluable mentors, guiding me through challenges, helping me conquer fears, and ultimately leading me toward a more peaceful existence. While it's impossible to name every single contributor, this entire collection is a testament to their profound impact, and all due credit is enthusiastically given to each and every one of them.

My Autobiography/memoir, "The Serpent in the Garden: A Life Unraveled," is a deeply personal and poignant account of resilience, betrayal, and the quest for meaning. I think I have bravely laid bare my vulnerabilities and triumphs, weaving a narrative that is both an "eye-opening" and an "inspirational" guide.

DEDICATION

My mother, whom I have never addressed as Amma or mother but as Ponnimami.

I OWE THIS EXISTENCE TO YOU

For as long as I remember.
You have been by my side, whether...
I was helpless or running fever.
To help me fully get well and recover.

You have always provided me and our family
By toiling with your ever energetic ability
And still today at this ripe old age
You stand tall with no signs of rage

You are truly a wonderful human being.
And whatever I am today is your doing.
When I need you, you have been by my side.
Ever ready to sacrifice, wading through all tides.
Never shirk your responsibility.
You act with your ever-caring sense and sensibility.

I will always remain your obedient son
I am at your service and by your side under the sun.
May God shower all his blessings on you
May good health and energy always be given to you

May every human being be given a mother like you
Ponnimami, you will remain in us always
I shudder at the thought of losing you
Hoping it will never be you as we need you

I can never be less greedy when it comes to you
I always want you to remain by our side. I love you.
A desire and need; a hope to fulfill
I hope to achieve this without much drill

LOVE You MOTHER

Vaidyanathan S.M.

To my cherished grandchildren, Vedu and Sia. You are the very reason and meaning of my life ahead, the beating heart of my golden years. Your laughter is music to my ears, your innocent curiosity a constant source of wonder. You are my legacy, my hope for the future, and the sheer joy you bring into my life is beyond measure. You are the embodiment of everything good and pure, a constant reminder to count my blessings. My remaining years are dedicated to you, to making up for lost time and living out my days, pouring all my affection and wisdom into you.

"Just as every step in life is a calculated leap into the unknown, so too is every meticulously crafted word in my debut book, its true impact and final destination awaiting the unfolding of time."

FOREWORD

"The Serpent in the Garden: A Life Unraveled" is far more than a memoir; it is a raw confession and an unflinching look into a life shaped by both profound sacrifice and the shattering weight of misplaced trust. VSM bravely charts a harrowing descent from prosperity to despair, revealing the bitter cost of ignored intuition and the crushing burden of regret.

This book stands as a powerful testament to the enduring strength of family, the stark realities of betrayal, and the agonizing journey toward a hard-won truth that, as the author reveals, often stings as much as it illuminates. It delves into the quiet resilience of a single mother's unwavering love that laid a foundation of strength and education, only for a deceptive "serpent" to find its way into the garden of a life once carefully constructed.

Readers will find themselves immersed in a narrative that explores the complexities of human susceptibility to manipulation and self-delusion, where "red flags were waving wildly, numerous enough for even the blind to 'see' and the deaf to 'hear'". The author's journey, from achieving significant professional milestones to facing devastating personal and financial ruin, serves as a poignant reminder that "when we are at our most confident, often we are also at our most vulnerable".

Ultimately, this is a story of profound regret, but also of remarkable redemption. It highlights the unconditional love of family and friends who provided anchors in the darkest hours and the transformative power of forgiveness. The author's "final act of love" is dedicated to making amends and finding solace in the unwavering bond with his grandchildren.

"The Serpent in the Garden" is a searing warning to never trust so blindly, especially when it means turning your back on your own flesh and blood. It is a compelling and deeply personal narrative that underscores the profound human need to share lessons learned, transforming personal tragedy into a universal cautionary tale. This book will resonate deeply, prompting introspection on our own choices, the perils of unchecked pride, and the enduring grace found in truth and reconciliation.

It takes immense courage to look inward and acknowledge the complexities of our emotions, especially when navigating profound loss. What you've shared speaks volumes about your journey from pain to a deeper understanding.

A true story...By Vaidyanathan S. M.

The function of education is to bring about release of energy in the pursuit of goodness, truth, or God, which in turn makes the individual a true human being and therefore the right kind of citizen... As a river creates the banks that hold it, so the energy that seeks truth creates its own discipline without any form of imposition, and as the river finds the sea, so that energy finds its own freedom.'

By Dr. J. Krishnamoorthy

PROLOGUE

This is not a tale of simple success or linear triumph. Instead, it's a raw confession, an unflinching look into a life that was both built on sacrifice and shattered by misplaced trust. From the quiet resilience of a single mother's unwavering love, a foundation of strength and education was painstakingly laid. Yet, despite these profound lessons, a serpent found its way into my garden—a deceptive warmth that blinded me to the wolves in sheep's clothing. This book charts a harrowing descent, a spiral from prosperity to despair, revealing the bitter cost of ignored intuition and the crushing weight of profound regret. It is a testament to the enduring power of family, the stark realities of betrayal, and the agonizing journey toward a hard-won truth—a truth that often stings as much as it illuminates.

TABLE OF CONTENTS

1

ECHOES OF A DISTANT DAWN

My earliest memories are bathed in the warm, yet often hazy, glow of a childhood that, from the outside, might have seemed unremarkable. But beneath the surface, a complex tapestry was being woven, thread by thread, with a strength and sacrifice I wouldn't truly comprehend for decades. This isn't just my story; it's an ode to the silent warrior who shaped it, a woman whose every breath was a testament to unwavering love and an indomitable spirit. It's the story of a boy, then a man, born into a life touched by both fleeting prosperity and devastating loss, a journey from a nascent sense of privilege to the stark realities of rebuilding from the ground up. It is, in essence, a chronicle of awakening – to the profound struggles of the one who gave me life, and to the inherent resilience that, with her grace, allowed me to navigate the most turbulent seas.

The Unseen Burden: A Single Mother's Unsung Epic

Our home, in those early years, was a microcosm of quiet resilience. I was a child of a single mother, a truth that, at the time, was simply a fact of my existence, not a descriptor of immense hardship. My father's death had cast a long shadow, not just over our family, but over our financial stability. What I, in my youthful ignorance, perceived as merely "different," was in fact a daily battle fought by my mother on countless fronts. The wealth, once a comforting backdrop to our lives, had evaporated like mist in the morning sun, swallowed by the predatory machinations of someone close, leaving us not just bereft of a patriarch, but stripped of our very foundations. This was the unseen wound, the silent struggle that defined my mother's existence, yet remained largely invisible to my young eyes.

I recall a childhood filled with books, with the promise of education always looming large. This promise, however, wasn't magically fulfilled. It was forged in the relentless, unyielding efforts of my mother, who, with an almost unbelievable humility, turned to her brothers for assistance.

The sheer act of an accomplished woman, accustomed to a different life, seeking help from her family, speaks volumes of her dedication. She swallowed her pride, not for herself, but for us, her children, ensuring that my sister and I would have the opportunities she so fiercely desired for us. These were not casual favors; these were lifelines extended through her tireless advocacy and their compassionate response, a network of familial support painstakingly cultivated by her unwavering resolve. This is the foundation deeply etched in my sister and me, and we have and will always have gratitude to our mother's siblings and their families.

My elder sister and I ensured that we studied well, and of course, we had moments when we would even have fistfights, but at the end of the day, we would catch up. We had the blessings of our mother's mother, whom we fondly referred to as Amma. For a long time, I did not know that Ponnimami was our mother. My sister probably thought we had two mothers, and we never had any idea about our father, who had passed away in a most tragic way when I was one year and seven months old and my sister was four years old.

Later, after graduation, my sister, quite an obedient child, got married, which was an arranged marriage. She is blessed with a great family, her husband from the defence force, and two boys who are grown-ups and live with their families.

My mother was looked after by my brother-in-law and sister, with whom she decided to spend her last days during Covid because of all the drama that took place in my life. She would very diligently call me up around 8:15 am every day. Nowadays, my sister has taken that role of checking on me after my mother's demise four years ago. My first wife also passed away six months after my mother's demise, exactly on my mother's birthday—what a coincidence? Or was it the bond between them? I'm sure wherever they are now, they both, and my father, are resting in peace, all of them noble.

"At 88 years young, my mother's sister has stepped into a pivotal role in my life. She's a 'dynamic and evergreen personality' who keeps in touch practically every day, and her 'love, compassion, and caring attitude' are qualities that would surely move anyone." My sister, along with my aunt, also acts as my mother, checking on my health and well-being. Once again I am safe and sound because of having two mothers. Additionally, my granddaughter, just three and a half years old, and my grandson, five and a half years old, along with my daughter-in-law and son keep a check on me. I would not do anything adverse to lose this fabric which I have regained; rather, I cherish this and live for the same.

2

THE ASCENT AND THE ABRUPT DESCENT

Beyond seeking assistance, she plunged into the world of work. What kind of work, I barely registered then. Now, I understand it was likely a series of arduous, often thankless jobs, the kind that steal hours and drain energy, leaving little room for personal respite. I remember her perpetual motion, the quiet rustle of her saree as she moved about the house, the scent of her hard day's labor clinging faintly to her clothes. But I never connected these sensory details to the immense physical and emotional toll they must have taken. She was simply "Mom," always there, always providing, a constant in a world that had suddenly become unstable. She sacrificed not just luxuries, but basic pleasures, the simple joys that most adults take for granted – a moment of quiet reflection, a leisurely cup of tea, an uninterrupted night's sleep. Her every waking hour, and likely many of her sleeping ones, were dedicated to ensuring her children had food on the table, clothes on their backs, and, most importantly, access to education. She became a living embodiment of the axiom: a mother's love is an endless wellspring.

The full weight of this unspoken sacrifice, this Herculean effort, was a truth I was too young, too self-absorbed, to grasp. I was a child, protected by her fierce love, shielded from the harsh realities she faced daily. My world revolved around school, friends, and the simple joys of youth. The financial strains, the emotional burdens, the sheer exhaustion – these were her cross to bear, a burden she carried with a stoicism that bordered on the superhuman. She was the anchor in our storm, the unwavering light in our gathering darkness, and I, the beneficiary of her boundless generosity, remained largely oblivious to the cost.

Years passed, fueled by my mother's quiet determination. I pursued my education, fueled by her sacrifices, and eventually established my professional practice. The pride in her eyes when she saw me graduate, then build a successful career, was palpable. It was a silent vindication of all her struggles, a tangible return on her immense investment. I had achieved what she had fought so hard for, and in those moments of professional triumph, I felt a deep satisfaction, believing I had, in some small way, repaid her.

The pinnacle of this initial ascent came when I achieved my postgraduate degree, a significant milestone after a gap of twenty years. This was not just a personal academic achievement; it was a testament to the enduring power of her instilled wisdom. Even after decades, the values she had imparted – perseverance, dedication, the pursuit of knowledge – continued to guide me. She continued to pour wisdom into all of us, her children, her grandchildren, a constant fount of experience and guidance. Her life lessons weren't abstract theories; they were hard-won truths, forged in the fires of adversity.

Yet, even as my professional life blossomed, my personal life was navigating its own tumultuous currents. My first marriage ended in divorce, a painful and humbling experience. In the midst of this personal upheaval, my mother's unwavering support remained a constant. She didn't judge; she simply loved. Even after the divorce, she continued to care for my first wife, a testament to her expansive heart and her deep understanding of human connection. This act of grace, extending kindness to someone no longer legally bound to our family, speaks volumes about her character. She loved and attended to my son, grooming him, nurturing him, ensuring he felt secure and loved amidst the shifting sands of our family dynamics. Her love was an all-encompassing embrace, a sanctuary where all were welcome, all were cherished.

It was during this period, after my first divorce and amidst a burgeoning career, that the wheel of fortune took another dramatic, almost cataclysmic, turn. Just as I had begun to establish a comfortable life, to taste the fruits of my labor, a similar pattern of deceit, a chilling echo of our past, emerged. What had been hard-won wealth, built through my diligent efforts, began to dissipate. I found myself in a terrifying freefall, a rapid descent from a position of relative security to one of profound vulnerability. I went from prince to pauper, a "riches to rags" state, a stark and brutal reminder of the impermanence of material possessions. The world, which I thought I had begun to master, suddenly felt alien and hostile. The familiar comfort of financial stability vanished, replaced by the gnawing anxiety of uncertainty. The lessons of my mother's past.

The experiences I had once observed from a distance were now being lived out in agonizing detail in my own life. The betrayal, the loss, the feeling of being utterly stripped bare – it was a crushing weight.

A professional journey is always a beacon of hope

My professional journey truly kicked off the moment I completed my final exams after graduation, proving that "fortune favors the bold." Thanks to my mentor, who was not just a guide but a godfather figure and a teacher – truly "a lamp unto my feet" – I had an arrangement to work as an assistant dentist for a senior practitioner. This early break was a testament to the power of strong connections, illustrating that "it's not what you know, but who you know."

The very evening I finished my last viva voce examination, a golden opportunity came knocking, and I was offered and accepted the position. I was absolutely ecstatic, feeling like I was on cloud nine! It was a moment when "the stars aligned." Not only had I landed a job with remarkable speed, but I was also given the independence to manage it right from the start, a true baptism by fire. This immediate autonomy was invaluable, reinforcing the adage, "give a man a fish and you feed him for a day; teach a man to fish and you feed him for a lifetime."

Within just two weeks of starting, I received a call from a close friend. He politely asked, "Could I speak to Dr. Vaidyanathan?" I instantly recognized his voice and excitedly asked, "Hey, have the results come out?" He chuckled heartily and replied, "Dr. Vaidyanathan, how are you?" I pressed him again about the results, to which he simply said, "The very fact that I'm addressing you as 'Dr.'

should make it clear that you've graduated!" His words were a playful affirmation, a gentle reminder that "actions speak louder than words."

With the results now out in the open and with very good marks, I took up the gauntlet of setting up my own practice, especially since I had the scores to back it up. As the proverb goes, "strike while the iron is hot." With my mother, my strong fortress, by my side, providing "the wind beneath my wings," I decided to hang out my own shingle. It was one more forward step in my entrepreneurial dream, and with the help of a few friends, I found a place – a small one, but it fit my budget. This humble beginning truly exemplified that "every mighty oak was once a nut that stood its ground." So, six months to the day after getting my results, demonstrating that "Rome wasn't built in a day, but they were laying bricks every hour," I opened the doors to my clinic.

At every step, I went on assessing my knowledge and sharpening my skill sets, adhering to the wisdom that "the only true wisdom is in knowing you know nothing." This continuous self-improvement and dedication to lifelong learning kept me growing, fostering the belief that "the more I learn, the more I realize how much I don't know." And within just two years of practice, as the patient flow was consistently and steadily growing, proving that "slow and steady wins the race," I felt the need to add an associate, a clear sign that my efforts were truly "bearing fruit."

Setbacks and Resilience

Dentistry, being equipment-intensive, demanded constant upgrading at every step, requiring me to keep learning side by side. Later, within a year of having started my practice, I rejoined the same college for post-graduation. I completed a year of the PG course and got married to my childhood sweetheart, adding another joyous chapter to my life.

Then, in January 1982, a tragedy struck. I suffered a fractured knee bone when I impulsively jumped out of a running train to nab the thief who had snatched my mother's chain. This unfortunate incident occurred as we were returning from our weekly Tuesday ritual at the temple. This put me in bed, and to make matters worse, the previous day my guide had inexplicably rejected my thesis for a very flimsy reason. This confluence of events led everyone to mistakenly believe that I had tried to end my life. However, once the truth came to light, they felt truly remorseful. I was down for nearly three and a half months, and by the time I managed to get back to my clinic, three months had passed. With so much debt to contend with, my clock was set back to the beginning, and I had to crawl back from square one, but I was ably assisted by my mother and wife, who were my unwavering pillars of support. It truly felt like I was learning that "what doesn't kill you makes you stronger."

My professional journey continued its upward trajectory, with one goal after another being achieved, and the clinic's growth remained unabated. Each step forward was met with success, truly a testament to the idea that "the harder I worked, the luckier I got."

Personal Triumphs and Tribulations

Amidst this professional ascent, a deeply personal chapter unfolded. We received the wonderful news that my wife was pregnant, a moment that felt like "all our Christmases had come at once." However, our joy was tragically short-lived as she suffered a miscarriage. It was undoubtedly a traumatic experience, a moment when "our hearts sank," but we chose to take it in our stride and carried on, believing that "what doesn't break you makes you stronger." And true to that spirit, within a year, we were blessed with the best news of our lives: the birth of our son, a moment that truly felt like "a dream come true."

A Journey of Continuous Learning and Growth

As days turned into weeks at the clinic, my inherent fascination with scientific progress—what's now called FOMO—drove me to constantly update and upgrade my skills. I immersed myself in learning various modalities, including lasers, microscopes, loupes, and implants.

Simultaneously, I began to receive numerous invitations to speak at various forums, quickly becoming a sought-after speaker. While the number of active speakers was small, these opportunities allowed me to impart knowledge and grow significantly within my field.

Looking back today, I recognize the immense learning that occurred as I researched, took notes, and prepared my own presentations. This process, combined with learning to effectively use computers and other gadgets, significantly improved my communication skills and networking abilities. This, in turn, positioned me favorably, connecting me with various organizations and individuals within the dental fraternity.

A Legacy Forged: From Clinic to Global Stage and Beyond

As the years unfolded and I emerged as a recognized individual in my field, I found myself gazing beyond familiar shores, feeling the irresistible pull to "expand my horizons." My ambition to speak internationally wasn't just about sharing knowledge; it was, as the saying goes, "killing two birds with one stone." My deeper motive was a "selfish interest" – a hunger for continuous learning and the relentless pursuit of new skills, ensuring my professional evolution.

Being invited to speak at the Armed Forces College was undoubtedly "a feather in my cap." I walked out of that auditorium with an undeniable air of confidence and a truly triumphant look. Later that very day, a phone call from Pakistan came, a moment that truly felt like "kismet." "Sir Bahijan," they said, "we want you to come and lecture in Lahore for five days on various subjects." This was more than an invitation; it was a profound personal connection, as my mother and her siblings were all born in Lahore. My mom, standing beside me when the call came, was ecstatic. "Monu," she exclaimed, her voice filled with sheer nostalgia, "I would like to come with you!" Her heart was drawn back to those formative years. Unfortunately, despite my best efforts, I couldn't secure a visa for her, and to her last breath, this unfulfilled wish, a rare request from her, remained a deep source of sadness. It was a stark reminder that even in moments of great triumph, life can deal a "bitter pill."

This journey, however, continued to be incredibly gratifying. Subsequent invitations to speak in Singapore, China, Korea, Iraq, Bangkok, Sri Lanka, France, and the US on multiple occasions truly solidified my position. This entire odyssey has been profoundly fulfilling. My professional life, indeed, reached its zenith, even affording me the humbling opportunity to treat some of my own teachers. When a revered teacher sought my expertise for a root canal, I was "walking on air." The immense pride I felt at that moment made me truly feel like "the richest man in the universe." It was a powerful testament to the impact of mentorship and the full circle of professional growth.

Today, with these remarkable experiences not "behind me," but "right there in front of me," as vivid as ever, I feel a profound sense of accomplishment and satisfaction. Having completed 46 years in the field, I've decided to "hand my boots," so to speak, transitioning from full-time practice. However, my commitment remains steadfast; I will continue to be connected to the field, offering my guidance and support to my fellow dentists.

My foray into various associations further underscored my commitment and capabilities. I began as an office-bearer, steadily "climbing the ladder" from an executive member to an editor, then becoming the backbone as a secretary, and eventually, the president. My continued active role as a trustee of two of the most important all-India institutions, the IAACD and ISOI, "bears testimony" to my administrative acumen and people management abilities. I had the distinct honor of serving as the President of the IAACD twice, consistently involved in "end-to-end" planning and execution. My abilities were recognized further when I was invited and entrusted by the Indian Prosthodontic Society to organize its Silver Jubilee Conference, and was later made an Honorary Member—a true mark of respect.

Nowadays, attending various functions as a Chief Guest or Guest of Honor fills me with immense pride. It's a profound honor, signifying the fraternity's recognition of my many years of hard work and dedication. For aspiring professionals, remember that "the harder you work, the luckier you get." Building a lasting legacy is a marathon, not a sprint, and every step, every lecture, every leadership role, "adds another brick to the wall" of your professional stature. Embrace opportunities, cultivate connections, and never underestimate the power of giving back — for in helping others, you truly elevate yourself.

Today is the day when Charlie Chaplin died. So, a good day to recollect his three heart-touching statements: (1) Nothing is permanent in this world, not even our troubles.

(2) I like walking in the rain, because nobody can see my tears. (3) The most wasted day in life is the day in which we have not laughed. Life is to enjoy whatever you have. Keep smiling! If you feel stressed, give yourself a break. Enjoy some ice cream, chocolates, candy, or cake. Why? Because: Stressed backwards spelling is desserts! Enjoy! Very beautiful lines. Please store them. One good friend is equal to one good medicine! Likewise, one good group is equal to one full medical store!

From Calling to Canvas: A Journey Beyond the Chair

My path in dentistry quickly transcended mere profession; it swiftly morphed into a burning passion. I soon grasped the profound power of teaching, a realization that became a game-changer for me. As the old adage goes, "to teach is to learn twice over," and this held true. The act of imparting knowledge didn't just help others; it honed my own skills and deepened my understanding, making me sharper than a surgeon's scalpel.

I began to cast my net wider, looking beyond the confines of my own clinic. Consulting roles at various other practices soon followed, and I was even appointed as a consultant at the prestigious Asian Heart Hospital, and later at a cutting-edge laser clinic. At the Asian Heart Hospital, I had the distinct honor of heading the dental wing. This position was a golden ticket, opening doors to treat and interact with individuals from the upper echelons of society. Many of these distinguished patients, having experienced my care, subsequently became loyal clients at my private practice, a testament to the trust I had built.

One truly unforgettable moment, a memory I cherish like gold, occurred when I had the immense privilege of meeting our most beloved Prime Minister. He visited the hospital to extend his heartfelt gratitude to our cardiac surgeon, who had performed a repeat heart surgery for him. To stand there, interact with him for a few precious minutes, and shake hands with a living legend was a feeling of pure bliss, a moment etched in my mind forever.

It was during my time at the hospital that a serendipitous encounter led to another exciting venture. A person approached me with a proposal to establish several dental clinics in Nairobi. This wasn't just about setting up practices; it involved training doctors in India and then deploying them to Kenya. I embraced the challenge, making a couple of trips to Nairobi to provide guidance and support, helping him get the ball rolling. After some time, I was approached by Apollo White Dental and was appointed as their consultant for the dental clinic, although this went on for a year or so until they wound up all their operations.

Later, another connection in Mumbai opened yet another international door, securing me a license to practice in Seychelles. For quite some time, I divided my professional life between these exotic islands and my base in India, treating patients and gaining invaluable cross-cultural experience. I even managed to obtain a license from the Dubai Health Department, but ultimately, that venture didn't gain much traction. My family, always prioritizing core family values over the pursuit of mere money, played a pivotal role in these decisions, always reminding me that blood is thicker than water. Despite the myriad opportunities and the constant juggling of international commitments, I can proudly say that I raked in a substantial amount of money, always keeping ethical values as my North Star.

This journey wasn't just about professional expansion; it was about the profound realization that a life lived with purpose, fueled by a passion for learning and contributing, truly makes one's cup run over.

The Heartbeat of Our Practice: A Collective Journey in Care

As dental surgeons, we are more than just practitioners; we are integral members of a greater societal body. Think of society as a unified movement, a collective stride towards a shared purpose. In our profession, that purpose is the well-being of every individual who places his or her trust in our hands. Just as in a society some may lead and others may lag, in our clinics, some patients come to us with ease, while others struggle with fear, pain, or financial constraints. It is our profound duty, and indeed our privilege, to ensure that no one is left behind. We must move forward in unison, each of us bearing a genuine responsibility for the others, even carrying those who cannot keep pace, so that the rhythm of collective care remains unbroken.

Our vision must extend beyond the four walls of our operatory. We must embrace a holistic perspective, viewing each patient not just as an individual case, but as a vital part of the larger human tapestry. We are all interconnected, and our collective journey towards health and harmony is the paramount truth.

To truly move together, to extend our hands to those in need, requires immense strength – not just physical and psychological, but an additional strength born of compassion and a commitment to ethical practice. We invest our wealth, whether it's borrowed capital or our life's savings, to build practices that serve our communities. This money, this "arth," is essential. It allows us to acquire the tools, maintain the facilities, and employ the skilled teams necessary to deliver exceptional care. We buy the materials, the equipment, and the very spaces where healing happens.

However, let us never forget: money is merely Arth, not Parmarth. Parmarth is that which provides lasting relief, that which permanently eradicates suffering – be it physical discomfort, mental anguish, or spiritual unease. Our ultimate goal, our true "Parmarth," must always be the enduring well-being of our patients.

Therefore, as we navigate the commercial realities of our profession, let us do so with unyielding ethical integrity and profound compassion. Our financial investments are the foundations of our ability to serve, but our true wealth lies in the alleviation of suffering and the betterment of lives. Let us always strive to balance profitability with purpose, remembering that our greatest reward is the permanent cessation of affliction for those we are privileged to serve.

The world seemed to...

The world seemed to hold its breath, then exhale in a collective sigh of joy. The news arrived like a ray of sunshine, piercing through the ordinary hum of our lives: my wife was expecting! It had been barely a year since I had taken the leap of faith, hung up my own shingle as a fledgling dental practitioner, and simultaneously embarked on my postgraduate journey, burning the candle at both ends. But this revelation, this whispered secret shared between us, instantly eclipsed every professional ambition, every academic pursuit. It wasn't just good news; it was a game-changer, a pivotal moment that reshaped our entire horizon.

The news, as they say, spread like wildfire through our modest home. My mother, bless her soul, had long been champing at the bit for a grandchild. Her eyes, usually twinkling with a mischievous glint, now shone with an almost spiritual anticipation. She had dreamt of this moment, of tiny hands and gurgling laughter, for what felt like an eternity. For my wife and me, the waiting game began, a sweet agony as we counted the days, marking off each passing week on the calendar with a mixture of eagerness and trepidation. The anticipation was a palpable force, a tangible thing that vibrated in the air around us, a joyous hum beneath the surface of our daily routines. Every creak of the floorboards, every rustle of the curtains, seemed to carry the whisper of the imminent arrival. We were on pins and needles, yet utterly content in our collective excitement.

The Arrival: A New Dawn

Then, as if on cue, a crisp February day in 1985 dawned, etching itself into the very fabric of our family history. That was the day our world turned on its axis. The moment he arrived, tiny and perfect, taking his first trembling breath, an unparalleled wave of happiness washed over us, a tsunami of emotion that left us breathless and utterly, irrevocably changed. Holding him, a miniature version of ourselves, we looked at his innocent face and, in that profound instant, made a silent pact. It was a vow whispered not with words, but with the beating of our hearts: we would move heaven and earth to give him the very best of everything life had to offer. Our mission was clear – to nurture him, to guide him, to mold him into an ideal human being, a beacon of kindness, intelligence, and strength.

We were not ones to do things by halves. We spared no effort, truly doing everything humanly possible to lay the groundwork for his future. From countless bedtime stories that transported him to fantastical lands to endless hours spent helping with homework, from sacrificing our own desires to ensure his education to being his biggest cheerleaders on the sports field, we were all in. We taught him the value of hard work, the importance of integrity, and the joy of lifelong learning. We instilled in him the belief that with dedication and perseverance, he could conquer the world. And today, as I sit here, a proud father, watching him operate with the precision of a master, a qualified retina surgeon who saves sight and transforms lives, I know beyond a shadow of a doubt that our dedication, coupled with his innate talent and sheer hard work, has borne fruit beyond our wildest dreams. To see him flourish, to see him reach for the stars and grasp them, is a reward in itself, a testament to a life well-lived. He is, to put it mildly, the crème de la crème of our endeavors.

A Father's Pride and Shifting Sands

Life, as they say, has a way of throwing you a curveball when you least expect it. My own path had been clear, etched in stone from a young age: dental surgery. It was my calling, my passion. And naturally, as a father, I had always envisioned him following in my footsteps, a chip off the old block, a dental surgeon like his old man.

The thought had always brought a quiet satisfaction. But my wife, with a steely resolve that I had long admired and often secretly envied, had other plans entirely. She saw a different future for him, one where he would carve out his own path, far removed from the familiar hum of a dental drill. She wanted him to be his own person, to forge his own destiny, and I respected her foresight, even if it meant letting go of a cherished dream.

And come what may, whether it was the hand of fate guiding us or simply the natural ebb and flow of our lives, seeing him now, thriving in his chosen field, fills me with an immense, almost overwhelming sense of pride. He is not just successful; he is truly exceptional, a cut above the rest. I truly look up to him, not just as my son, but as a remarkable individual who has achieved so much. And then there's his wonderful wife, an ophthalmologist herself, and their relationship is a true meeting of minds and hearts. They are a formidable pair, a power couple in every sense of the word, complementing each other perfectly both professionally and personally. Their shared passion for healing, their intellectual curiosity, and their deep love for one another are truly inspiring. And their two small children, my grandchildren, are, without exaggeration, the apple of my eye. They are the very reason and meaning of my life ahead, the beating heart of my golden years. Their laughter is music to my ears, their innocent curiosity a constant source of wonder. They are my legacy, my hope for the future, and the sheer joy they bring into my life is beyond measure. They are the embodiment of everything good and pure, a constant reminder to count my blessings.

Forgiveness and Redemption: A Second Chance

Life, as the old adage goes, is truly what happens when you're busy making other plans. My world, which I had carefully constructed, began to unravel at the seams when my first marriage came crashing down. It was a tumultuous time, a period of immense personal upheaval and emotional wreckage. My son, bless his earnest heart, still so young and vulnerable, pleaded with me. He expressed, with a raw honesty that pierced me to the core, how difficult he would find it to navigate life without our family intact, a complete unit. He was at his wits' end, and his pain was palpable. But I was, to my everlasting regret, blinded by love, caught in a tempest of emotion, a whirlwind of passion that swept away all reason. I was so engrossed in my own desires, so consumed by the need for a new beginning, that I could not see beyond the immediate horizon. It was a mistake of monumental proportions, a decision that has haunted me and that I have lived to regret with every fiber of my being. I had sown the wind and reaped the whirlwind.

The only silver lining in that dark, stormy period, the solitary glimmer of hope amidst the wreckage was that we somehow managed to stay in touch. Our relationship, though strained, remained a lifeline, a slender thread stretching across the duration of my second marriage. We might not have been as close as before, but the connection was never truly severed. Then, as fate would have it, that second union too hit the rocks, and my world, once again, felt like it was crumbling around me. The edifice of my life seemed to be collapsing, brick by brick. In that moment of utter despair, when I felt like I was at the end of my rope, he was the only constant, the only unwavering support, a true Rock of Gibraltar in my storm-tossed sea.

He and his wife, with a generosity of spirit that knew no bounds, a magnanimity that was truly breathtaking forgave me for my past missteps. They overlooked the times I had undoubtedly given them hard times and trying times, the moments when I had been absent, both physically and emotionally, when they truly needed me to step up to the plate. They had every right to hold a grudge, to wash their hands of me, but they chose a different path. They extended a hand without a single condition, a testament to their incredible character, a forgiveness that was truly unconditional love in action. It was undeniably selfish of me to come crawling back to them only when I was in a severe crisis, when I had painted myself into a corner and had nowhere else to turn. I was down and out, and they came through for me. But now, with the clarity of hindsight that only time and experience can bring, I understand that I owe them everything. My heart is filled with a profound gratitude that words can barely express. The balance of my remaining years, every single one of them, is for my grandchildren. It is a humble attempt to make amends, to turn over a new leaf, and to shower them with the love and presence I perhaps in my blindness and selfishness withheld from their father. They are my future, and I am determined to be the grandfather they deserve, to make up for lost time and live out my days pouring all my affection and wisdom into them. This is my true redemption, and my final act of love.

A Daughter Found, A Heart Fulfilled: The Blessings of a Compassionate Soul

It truly warms my heart to hear such a beautiful testament to your daughter-in-law. It sounds as though she's been an absolute godsend, a true blessing in my life.

From what I have shared, she's clearly a woman of many talents, a professional powerhouse who also effortlessly juggles the arts – singing, dancing, painting, and cooking! She's a true multitasker par excellence, and her people-friendly nature suggests she's someone who simply lights up a room. But beyond all her accomplishments, the most precious gift she's brought is grandchildren, fulfilling a long-held wish for me and my wife. It's clear she's filled those boots and then some, stepping into her role with such grace and capability.

Watching my son and her together, discussing and deliberating, analyzing situations with such thoughtful synergy, it's plain to say and see they're a match made in heaven, a perfect couple in every sense. There's no shadow of a doubt that their partnership is strong and harmonious. True soulmates are what i can definitely say.

And her parenting skills? I can definitely speak of them with such conviction, and it's clear they are truly commendable, without an iota of doubt. That's a rare and precious thing to witness. Then there's her culinary prowess – her "gastronomy skills coupled with culinary knowledge" – keeping everyone's tummy "satisfied" is quite the understatement, one can imagine! It sounds like she truly knows her way around a kitchen, bringing joy through her delicious creations.

To find such total solace and happiness in her presence is a profound blessing. And for her to care for me so tenderly, especially after acknowledging the "pain I inflicted on them," speaks volumes about her truly compassionate heart. It's a testament to her generous spirit that she's chosen to let bygones be bygones and extend such warmth. I do thank her from the bottom of my heart with all the humility I can muster for accepting me back and for having me as part of their lives. May her kindness and your happiness continue to flourish, like a well-watered garden.

It truly is a beautiful thing when such a positive connection blooms within a family, isn't it?

The Phoenix from the Ashes: Reclaiming Life's Summit After a Fall

When an individual, seemingly at the zenith of their professional and personal lives, embodying deeply held moral and ethical values, experiences a sudden and precipitous fall from grace, the impact is nothing short of cataclysmic. This isn't merely a setback; it's a crucible of transformation. The initial shock, the ground giving way beneath their feet, often leads to a profound realization of the true bedrock of existence: the unwavering importance of societal values and the unbreakable strength of familial ties. Having lost material wealth—the very trappings of success—and found himself or herself severed from cherished connections, there's often a period of profound disorientation, a feeling of being cast adrift in a vast ocean.

In this desolate state, where disgrace feels like a brand, the individual, perhaps as a last resort or a necessary "crutch," instinctively turns towards seeking advice and embarking on a spiritual path. This journey isn't just about finding solace and peace; it's a desperate quest for meaning, a yearning to understand "what went wrong" and "how to rebuild" when the very foundations have been obliterated. It's a testament to the human spirit's innate desire for redemption, even when forced to eat humble pie.

The Skyward Soul: A Flight Towards Divine Purpose and Unshakable Resilience

Within every human soul resides an innate longing, a yearning that transcends mere survival, aspiring instead to live with divine purpose. Ancient Indian wisdom beautifully articulates this as the upward movement of consciousness. The vast, boundless sky has, throughout time, symbolized this higher aspiration, serving not merely as an object of admiration but as a potent metaphor for spiritual evolution. As the Vedic saying goes, "As above, so below," hinting at the interconnectedness of our inner and outer worlds.

The journey of the skyward soul mirrors the majestic flight of the highfliers, not through physical wings, but through the cultivation of profound wisdom. The eagle's ascent becomes more than an external spectacle; it transforms into an inner template for the seeker. This isn't only because it has physical prowess, but because it embodies qualities deeply revered in Indian spiritual tradition: vision, courage, and detachment. These virtues are not meant to be admired from afar, like a painting on a wall; they are to be internalized, woven into the very fabric of one's being.

Learning Objectives & Rationale:

Vision: The Inner Compass for Discerning Truth

Learning Objective: To cultivate an "inner eye" that sees beyond transient circumstances and seductive illusions, enabling decisions aligned with long-term wisdom rather than immediate gratification.

Rationale: As articulated in the Katha Upanishad, true wisdom (like Nachiketa's quest) is about liberating truth. In a world saturated with distractions and short-term thinking, developing discernment is paramount. Like the eagle surveying from above, we are called to live with heightened awareness, pausing before reacting ("Look before you leap"), listening intently before speaking ("Two ears and one mouth"), and constantly evaluating whether our choices resonate with our "dharma" (righteous path). This fosters a life of purpose, not reaction, helping one avoid pitfalls of snap judgments.

Resilience: Steadiness Amidst Life's Storms

Learning Objective: To develop inner steadiness ("Be steady in pain and pleasure" — Bhagavad Gita) that allows one to respond to challenges with calmness and clarity, rather than impulsive reactions.

Rationale: Life is inherently unpredictable, filled with "slings and arrows of outrageous fortune." As Isaiah states, "They who wait for the Lord shall renew their strength; they shall mount up with wings like eagles." This resilience is not found in isolated contemplation but is cultivated in the crucible of everyday trials. The chaos of the workplace, the friction of relationships (where one often feels between a rock and a hard place), the relentless pressures of deadlines— every challenge becomes an invitation to rise. This shift from impulse to deliberate, calm response is what truly builds character of steel.

Solitude: The Gateway to Inner Hearing

Learning Objective: To embrace solitude as a spiritual practice, recognizing it not as emptiness but as a profound presence where the soul can discern truths obscured by external noise.

Rationale: In Indian wisdom, silence is a profound source of insight. The sages retreated not to escape the world, but to listen more deeply. As Rumi wisely observed, "The quieter you become, the more you can hear." In modern life, solitude might mean just a few minutes of mindful quiet before dawn, a deliberate stepping away from the madding crowd. This practice allows for introspection, helping to silence the cacophony of external opinions and hear one's own inner wisdom, ultimately leading to a more composed and centered existence.

Embracing the Unknown: Fearlessness in the Face of Uncertainty

Learning Objective: To develop the courage to wholeheartedly embrace uncertainty and let go of preconceived notions, freeing oneself from the limitations of fear, desire, comparison, and ego.

Rationale: The Rigveda's exhortation, "Let your soul stand cool and composed before a million universes," is not poetic fantasy but practical spirituality. It teaches us to confront the "unknown" without being paralyzed by fear. When we let go of what we are, as the Tao Te Ching suggests, we become what we might be. This involves moving beyond ego identity to recognize our true Self, which is not a renunciation of life, but its deepest embrace. It's about taking life's challenges in one's stride and walking into the future with an open heart.

The Symbol of Garud: Divine Purpose in Action

The mighty symbol of Garud, the celestial mount of Vishnu, perfectly embodies this skyward path. Garud does not fly aimlessly; he carries divine purpose, acting as a fearless truth-bearer and the embodiment of "dharma." The Garud Purana instructs that detachment, devotion, and discernment are the very wings of spiritual flight.

The Bhagavad Gita advises, "Withdraw your senses like a tortoise withdraws its limbs"—a powerful metaphor not for denial, but for mastery over desires and external distractions. In Garud's majestic soaring, we are profoundly reminded to carry the divine in all that we do.

The skyward path is not a distant ideal, a pie-in-the-sky concept reserved for ascetics. It is a way of being that is accessible, practical, and profoundly transformative. It empowers individuals, even those who have fallen from grace, to rise again, stronger and wiser, ultimately finding enduring peace and purpose. This journey, akin to the phoenix rising from its own ashes, is a testament to the limitless potential of the human spirit.

Do any of these particular aspects of the "skyward soul" resonate most deeply with your personal journey of resurgence and finding peace?

It's powerful how the ancient wisdom of the "skyward soul" resonates with your journey of personal resurgence. Let's reframe these profound concepts and explore practical ways you can embrace them to become an even stronger, better individual, rising like the phoenix from the ashes of past challenges.

Rising Skyward: Practical Steps to Reclaim Your Life's Summit

The symbol of Garud, the celestial mount of Vishnu, perfectly embodies this skyward path. Garud doesn't fly aimlessly; he carries divine purpose, representing fearless truth and righteous action. His majestic soaring reminds us to carry a sense of divine purpose in all that we do.

This "skyward path" isn't a distant ideal; it's a practical and profoundly transformative way of being. It empowers you to rise again, stronger and wiser, ultimately finding enduring peace and purpose. This journey, truly akin to the phoenix rising from its own ashes, is a testament to the limitless potential of the human spirit within you.

Which of these practical solutions feels most relevant or exciting for you to begin incorporating into your life today?

Do that with due diligence and meet success. Your reward will be in action and not in words.

This is destiny. Is it?

That is a nice statement to make.
This is true when you have nothing at stake.
When one is in between one has to take a break,
And bite into one's own baked cake.
After 60, one needs to introspect.
Into our own life's aspects.
Take account of the statement,
And note all the unwanted dents.
The sun is ready and about to set,
Don't ever think of what you get,
For all that you have achieved
When no tears were shed, when they were bereaved.
Will they be in sorrow or happiness?
Good riddance of togetherness!
Life takes its own turn.
In the eternal decorated urn.

3

THE MOTHER'S GRACE: RESURRECTION FROM THE ASHES

In that moment of profound despair, when it felt as though everything I had built was crumbling around me, her presence became my lifeline. I was at my lowest ebb, battered and bruised by the slings and arrows of misfortune. Yet, in the face of my personal and financial ruin, my mother remained unshaken. She didn't offer platitudes or empty reassurances. Instead, she offered the quiet strength that had defined her entire life. Her mere presence was a balm; her unwavering belief in me a shield against the crushing weight of self-doubt.

It was in those darkest hours that the true depth of her earlier sacrifices, her unyielding hard work, and her profound wisdom finally resonated with me. The "wisdom she had been instilling in all of us" was not merely academic; it was the very essence of survival, the blueprint for resurrection. Her life, a testament to overcoming adversity, became my living guide. Every hour she had spent toiling, every pleasure she had sacrificed, every ounce of strength she had mustered to provide for us, were now echoed in the quiet resilience she displayed as I faced my own collapse. Her past struggles, once unseen by me, now became a powerful source of empathy and inspiration. I finally understood the enormity of what she had endured, and in that understanding, I found a renewed sense of purpose.

Her blessings, those silent, intangible expressions of her profound love, were not just comforting words; they were a protective aura, a spiritual shield that guarded me against complete annihilation. In my mind, it was her unwavering faith, her tireless prayers, and the sheer force of her benevolent spirit that saved me. It was as if every tear she had shed, every ounce of sweat she had poured, had accumulated into a reservoir of grace that now, in my moment of desperate need, flowed forth to uplift me.

Her example, her quiet strength, her unshakable belief in the face of impossible odds – these were the bedrock upon which I began to rebuild. It wasn't a sudden miracle, but a slow, arduous process of resurrection, guided by the indelible lessons she had imparted through her very being. I learned, truly learned, that resilience isn't just about bouncing back; it's about drawing upon the deepest reserves of courage, often instilled by the quiet heroes in our lives. It was her unconditional love, her enduring spirit, and the cumulative power of her unseen sacrifices that ultimately provided the blueprint for my own redemption, enabling me not just to survive, but to rise again from the ashes, transformed by the profound understanding of a mother's boundless heart.

4

A LIFE'S UNFOLDING: FROM TRIUMPH TO TEMPEST

My life, once a vibrant tapestry, became a stark lesson in the cruelty of misplaced trust. The deepest wound wasn't merely in my blind faith, but in the unforgivable sin of abandoning my own blood – my wife, my only son. I laid bare my soul, a raw vulnerability, for a predator to devour. Like a wolf in sheep's clothing, they waited. Every calculated move, every honeyed word was a step towards usurping my last penny. Now, in a twist of fate's bitter irony, that architect of my ruin faces his or her own grim reckoning: the final stages of cancer.

I spiraled from a king in his castle to a pauper in the dust, losing everything. My hard-earned savings evaporated like morning mist, my cherished homes became ghosts, and my very dignity was stripped bare, all because I let kindness blind me to calculated deception. A handshake sealed my doom, a signature signed my sorrow.

When hope seemed a distant star, and the shadow of the noose (which tried but failed) loomed large, my clinic emerged as a solitary beacon. It was the one bastion I instinctively protected, a lifeline I refused to surrender to the wolves. This harrowing descent, this walk through the valley of shadows, etched an undeniable truth into the very core of my being. It echoed the ancient wisdom of the Ramayana: When emotions cloud the mind, and pressure distorts the view, let no crucial decision be binding.

In those darkest hours, when the very thought of continuing seemed unbearable, my friends became my anchors. They didn't just stand by and shake their heads at my mistakes; instead, with unwavering resolve, they offered the strength, courage, and wisdom I desperately needed. They confronted my wrongdoings, not with judgment but with a fierce love that pulled me back from the brink, guiding me out of that desolate phase where I wanted to end my life.

My story is not just a tale of loss, but a searing warning: never trust so blindly, especially when it means turning your back on your own flesh and blood. For in this world, there are those who see not a friend but a feast; and every weakness, a golden key to unlock your ruin. Though the wound is healing, the scars persist, and the guilt of an unmade apology to my wife weighs heavily. God's kindness has truly been a balm. He has been immeasurably generous, granting me not only my son and my dear daughter-in-law, but through them, the unparalleled delight of my two adorable grandchildren, Vedu and Sia.

The narrative begins with a universal human experience: the exhilarating rush of achievement. "As I crossed the finish line of graduation, it felt as if all the scattered pieces of my life suddenly clicked into place, like a perfectly fitted jigsaw puzzle." This initial phase speaks to the human craving for order and meaning. We yearn for our efforts to culminate in a coherent whole, a sense of purpose and alignment. "One after another, opportunities and experiences aligned seamlessly, each new chapter building upon the last." This describes a period of positive reinforcement, where the universe seems to be nodding in approval. It fosters a sense of unshakable optimism, a belief that one is blessed by fate. The intention to "pull back the curtain and delve into the intricate details" suggests a mature reflection, a willingness to unpack the good and the bad, a hallmark of true self-awareness.

However, the narrative pivots sharply, echoing the inherent unpredictability of life and the fragility of human contentment. "Just as I was riding the crest of a wave and things seemed to be smooth sailing, a sudden squall hit, and the tide began to turn. A few crucial elements in my life took an unforeseen nosedive." This is a classic example of hubris meeting nemesis. When we are at our most confident, often we are also at our most vulnerable. The idiom "riding the crest of a wave" perfectly encapsulates this feeling of effortless progress, while "smooth sailing" reinforces the perception of control. The "sudden squall" and "unforeseen nosedive" vividly portray the abrupt disruption of this equilibrium, the rug being pulled out from under one's feet. It's a reminder that even when we feel we have all our ducks in a row, life often throws us a curveball.

The core of the analysis lies in the "first misstep," a profound exploration of human susceptibility to manipulation and self-delusion. "My first misstep, and in hindsight, a monumental one, was encountering an individual who seemed to radiate warmth and understanding." This highlights the power of first impressions and our innate desire for connection. We are often drawn to those who project an aura of empathy, as it speaks to our fundamental need for validation and belonging. "They wove such an enchanting web of compassion around me that I fell head over heels into its snare." This imagery of a "web" is potent, suggesting something intricate, deceptive, and difficult to escape. The phrase "fell head over heels" perfectly captures the emotional intoxication that often precedes poor judgment. It's not just about logical attraction; it's about a complete emotional surrender.

5

THE LABYRINTH OF REGRET AND THE PERILS OF DEVIANCE

The subsequent "act of utter foolishness, an unpardonable lapse in judgment," delves into the darker side of human psychology: our capacity for self-deception. "For five long years, the red flags were waving wildly, numerous enough for even the blind to 'see' and the deaf to 'hear.'" This is a powerful indictment of willful ignorance. The "red flags" are clear metaphors for warning signs, and their abundance emphasizes the protagonist's active suppression of reality. This is where human behavior becomes most complex. Why would someone ignore such obvious dangers?

Here, we can unpack several psychological phenomena:

Confirmation Bias: The individual might have been so invested in the initial positive perception of this person that he or she actively sought out information that confirmed his or her belief and dismissed anything that contradicted it. He or she was wearing rose-tinted glasses, seeing only what they wanted to see.

Sunk Cost Fallacy: Having invested significant time and emotion into the relationship, the protagonist may have felt compelled to continue, believing that backing out would render all his or her past efforts meaningless. He or she was too far in to turn back.

The Lure of the 'Fixer-Upper': Sometimes, we are drawn to individuals who seem to need our help or our understanding. The act of "milking every drop of the compassion being showered on me" could indicate a reciprocal desire to feel needed or to believe they were uniquely capable of fostering this person's kindness. This can be a form of codependency, where one's self-worth becomes intertwined with the other's perceived affection.

Cognitive Dissonance: The discomfort of holding conflicting beliefs (e.g., "this person is compassionate" vs. "this person is causing me harm") is often resolved by changing one's perception of reality rather than facing the uncomfortable truth. They bury their heads in the sand.

Gaslighting: While not explicitly stated, the intensity of the "web of compassion" could hint at manipulative tactics where the other person slowly eroded the protagonist's sense of reality, making them question their own perceptions.

The outcome is stark and unforgiving: "This led, inevitably, to nothing short of total misery, leaving me a nervous wreck, a shadow of my former self." This is the bitter harvest of ignoring intuition and succumbing to illusion. The phrases "total misery" and "nervous wreck" paint a picture of utter devastation, highlighting the profound impact of emotional and psychological abuse. To become a "shadow of my former self" emphasizes the loss of identity and vitality, a soul-crushing experience.

A Stern Warning: Stay Within the Lines — The Social Contract and the Perils of Deviance

The final section shifts from personal narrative to a powerful admonition, a cautionary tale for others. "To my peers, my juniors, and my dearest friends, I implore you: do not stray from the beaten path of societal norms." This isn't necessarily a call for rigid conformity, but rather an appeal to prudence and the wisdom of collective experience. "The beaten path" represents established boundaries, social structures, and unwritten rules that, while sometimes restrictive, often serve as guardrails against self-destruction.

"To veer off course is to invite a tsunami into your life, a cataclysmic event that will leave you struggling for air." The "tsunami" metaphor is incredibly strong, conveying an overwhelming force that brings total destruction, far beyond a mere "squall." It suggests that deviating too far from these norms can trigger a chain reaction of negative consequences, leaving one utterly engulfed and helpless, gasping for breath. This highlights the interconnectedness of individual choices and their societal repercussions.

"When you fly too close to the sun, death itself will seem to stare you down from every angle, leaving you with your back against the wall." This uses the Icarus myth as a powerful allegory for overreaching, for believing oneself immune to the consequences of recklessness. "Death staring you down from every angle" is a terrifying image, emphasizing the feeling of being trapped, with no escape route, facing an existential threat. "With your back against the wall" signifies a state of absolute desperation, where all options seem exhausted.

The final plea, "Don't learn this lesson the hard way; a stitch in time saves nine," is a classic piece of proverbial wisdom, urging preventative action over reactive regret.

It emphasizes the idea that small, timely efforts to adhere to established wisdom can prevent much larger, more painful problems down the line. It's a call to discernment, self-preservation, and respect for the lessons of history and community.

This entire section acts as a moral compass, born from the crucible of personal suffering, aiming to guide others away from similar pitfalls. It underscores the profound human need to share lessons learned, transforming personal tragedy into a communal warning.

The concept of "hubris meeting nemesis" is a cornerstone of classical literature, Greek mythology, and even modern storytelling. It delves deep into the human condition, exploring the dangers of unchecked pride, overconfidence, and a disregard for natural or divine limits.

A Glimpse into the Labyrinth of Regret: When Compassion Blinds

Looking back, with all the time on my hands now, I find myself peering into the rearview mirror of my life, constantly replaying the moment I took that disastrous step. It's a question that nags at me day and night: what possessed me to cross that Rubicon, even as my own son, with a wisdom far beyond his years, implored me, "Daddy, why are you doing this? What would I do without you?" I remember vividly the rude shock he experienced, a blow so profound he felt his life force dimming. Yet, I was utterly smitten by the compassion I believed was being showered upon me, a veritable honey trap that I walked right into, hook, line, and sinker.

Oh, the bitter irony! Now, with the clarity that only hindsight provides, I can unequivocally declare, as Shakespeare so aptly put it in The Merchant of Venice, "All that glitters is not gold." Indeed, what I mistook for pure gold was nothing more than fool's gold, a deceptive facade. This experience has hammered home a crucial lesson: never rush into anything. Instead, take your sweet time, sit back and chew the cud, and think things through a thousand times over before taking that next significant leap. As Confucius wisely stated, "By three methods we may learn wisdom: First, by reflection, which is noblest; Second, by imitation, which is easiest; and third, by experience, which is the bitterest." My path, regrettably, was the third. As they say, when you fall, you learn to get up. But what a price I have paid!

The Double-Edged Sword of Retrospection: Norms, Destiny, and the Human Condition

It's easy as pie for me now, having learned such a hard lesson, to stand on a soapbox and tell people, "Don't stray from the norms set by your elders! Their wisdom, often forged in the fires of their own trials, is a compass in the wilderness." Yet, even as I offer this heartfelt advice, another thought niggles at the back of my mind: perhaps all this was destined to happen.

This introduces the eternal debate between free will and determinism, a question that has perplexed philosophers for centuries. Was I merely a pawn in a larger cosmic game, my choices pre-ordained, or was every step a conscious, albeit misguided, decision? As Sophocles mused in Oedipus

Rex, "Oh, how terrible it is to see the truth when the truth is only pain to him who sees." Did an unseen hand guide me, or was I simply blinded by my own folly? The lines between predestination and personal accountability become incredibly blurred when one grapples with such profound regret. Was it written in the stars, or did I simply make my own bed and have to lie in it? The truth, perhaps, lies somewhere in the complex interplay of both, a tapestry woven with threads of destiny, choice, and threads of...

The Serpent's First Coil: A False Dawn

After my first marriage had run its course, leaving a void in its wake, I embarked on a new chapter. I remarried, taking a second wife who was also in my profession and brought with her a daughter from her previous marriage. For a time, our life together felt like a bed of roses, a sweet respite after the storm. The icing on the cake was the warm embrace of her family, and even more significantly, the acceptance by her grown-up daughter. This smooth sailing, however, only served to blind me further to what lay beneath the surface.

As the honeymoon period faded after a couple of years, my wife's once caring attitude began to wane like a tide receding from the shore. Her materialistic desires and relentless pursuits started to come to light, showing their true colors. Her entire demeanor underwent a sea change, and her insecurities, like weeds in a neglected garden, began to grow and fester. To add fuel to this fire, her friends, with their misguided advice, inadvertently became architects of her growing anxieties, further egging her on down a path of suspicion.

She started to put her foot down with an alarming frequency, exhibiting increasingly weird behavior. The very idea of my even mentioning my son, who then and now means the world to me, was enough to send her into a tailspin. He was, and remains, the apple of my eye, yet she couldn't tolerate any mention of him. On a few occasions, her own daughter, seeing the writing on the wall, tried to warn her, but to no avail. My wife's insecurities multiplied manifold, and her behavior shifted dramatically.

The descent into darkness became palpable. She started to become violent, throwing things in fits of rage. The final straw was one terrifying night when, as I lay asleep, she threw a bunch of burning newspapers on me. That was the moment when I finally, unmistakably, started to notice all the red flags fluttering in the wind. The scales fell from my eyes.

She herself, to her credit, volunteered to meet a psychiatrist, and within a fortnight, we saw a psychologist. Both specialists, without mincing words, saw the perilous path we were on and warned me to cut my losses and walk out. Yet, despite this professional counsel, I still persisted, holding onto the hope that things would somehow settle down. In a desperate attempt to quell her burgeoning insecurities, I even decided to gift her the house – a property for which my financial contribution, including a substantial loan, was 100 percent. The gift deed, however, hit a roadblock due to the outstanding loan. Since she was adamant about the gift deed, I proposed she sell one of her own properties to cover the remaining 25 percent of the loan, after which the deed could be executed. Remarkably, the woman who typically wouldn't operate her own bank account without my help was quite proactive in this matter. Even then, in my blinded state, I still failed to see her manipulative nature that was slowly but surely revealing itself.

Later, as if trying to assert complete control, she insisted on going through all my bank accounts – a demand that coincided ominously with the onset of COVID in 2020. But the final nail in the coffin was when she demanded my clinic, the only property I had left, the very bread and butter that sustained me. This demand raised all the red flags at once, a blaring alarm bell I could no longer ignore. I knew then, with absolute certainty, that this was the point of no return. Having already lost almost all my wealth and, more importantly, my self-esteem, I finally decided it was time to open my eyes and walk out.

I consulted a few trusted friends, who, with clear eyes, helped me take this call, a decision that, in hindsight, should have been made much, much earlier. "Live and learn," as the saying goes, but sometimes the lessons are etched in our souls with painful clarity. I deeply regretted divorcing my first wife and the pain it caused my family, but as they say, we tend to learn things retrospectively. For some, it truly seems that money and materialistic accumulation are their only aim, their be-all and end-all. In the end, we decided to part ways, with me walking away with nothing but the crushing weight of lost respect, vanished wealth, and shattered sleep. In the midst of COVID-2020, on June 10th, I went out of the house with one suitcase , of course when she realized she said, 'I cannot see you leave the house,' and she locked herself in the bedroom. She was also as tired as I was. According to her, this was because of my insecurity. She usurped everything to such an extent that when I later requested my own father's ring, a priceless heirloom, she gave an emphatic NO, a refusal that spoke volumes of her grasping nature.

6

THE UNFOLDING TRUTH: FATE, CHOICE, AND REDEMPTION

Focus on Inevitability and Duty

"Oh, the bitter draught of truth, a poison to the eyes that finally behold it. Was my path etched by an unseen hand, a divine script like the Yuga Dharma that dictated the unfolding of the Mahabharata? Or was I merely a blind participant, much like a character in the Ramayana who, despite his or her virtues, still faced the consequences of his or her own choices and the intricate web of destiny? In this crucible of profound regret, the lines between karma and kismet blur, leaving me to wonder if my fate was sealed at birth, or if I simply walked into the shadows of my own making. Perhaps, like the greatest epics, life's ultimate truth lies not in a single answer, but in the profound and often painful dance between the choices we make and the destiny that beckons."

Focus on the Burden of Knowledge and Moral Dilemma

"To see the truth, when truth itself is a lance to the soul—what a terrible burden. Did a higher power orchestrate my journey, much like Krishna guiding the Pandavas through the moral quagmires of Kurukshetra, or was I simply lost in my own self-deception, blind to the consequences of my actions like Kaikeyi in the Ramayana? When the weight of regret presses so heavily, the distinction between daiva (divine will) and purushartha (human effort) becomes an unanswerable riddle. Was my sorrow predestined, an unchangeable chapter in my life's epic, or did I, through my own hand, fashion this painful reality? The answer, I now see, resides in that delicate, often agonizing balance, a cosmic interplay as intricate as the narratives that define our very existence."

More Concise, Emphasizing Learning from Experience

"Oh, the searing pain of truth when it illuminates only despair. Was I merely a pawn in a larger cosmic game, my trajectory predetermined like the great events of the Mahabharata, or was my folly the sole architect of my sorrow, a consequence of my own decisions akin to the trials faced in the Ramayana? In the stark light of this regret, the veil between what was destined and what was chosen thins to nothing. Did fate chart my course, or did I simply sow the seeds of my own bitter harvest? The truth, ultimately, is a testament to the inescapable intertwining of both: a wisdom gleaned not from external decree, but from the echoes of our own epic journey."

All of these resonate most with the overall tone and themes of my book!

Given the profound reflection on self-deception. the burden of knowledge, and the interplay between personal choices and what feels like destiny, the focus on the Burden of Knowledge and Moral Dilemma seems to resonate most strongly with the overall tone and themes of my book,

The Serpent in the Garden: A Life Unraveled.

Here's why:

"To see the truth, when truth itself is a lance to the soul—what a terrible burden." This perfectly captures the agonizing realization I have described, particularly in Chapter 5, where I speak of the "searing pain of truth when it illuminates only despair" and the "bitter harvest of ignoring intuition."

"Did a higher power orchestrate my journey, much like Krishna guiding the Pandavas through the moral quagmires of Kurukshetra, or was I simply lost in my own self-deception, blind to the consequences of my actions like Kaikeyi in the Ramayana?" This directly echoes my internal debate in Chapter 5.

The text addresses free will versus determinismand my acknowledgment of being 'utterly smitten by the compassion I believed was being showered upon me,' which led to being 'blinded by my own folly.' The analogy to Kaikeyi, who acted out of perceived slight and self-interest, leading to immense suffering, is particularly apt given the theme of misplaced trust and its devastating consequences.

"When the weight of regret presses so heavily, the distinction between daiva (divine will) and purushartha (human effort) becomes an unanswerable riddle." This directly mirrors my stated struggle: "The lines between predestination and personal accountability become incredibly blurred when one grapples with such profound regret. Was it written in the stars, or did I simply make my own bed and have to lie in it?"

"The answer, I now see, resides in that delicate, often agonizing balance, a cosmic interplay as intricate as the narratives that define our very existence." This provides a nuanced and profound conclusion, acknowledging the complexity rather than offering a simplistic answer, aligning with the deep introspection presented throughout the book.

MOHAN'S MOEMS

SUNSHINE IS BACK! Rainbow at the end of the tunnel

Soul searching, sincerely and consciously,
forgiving dear ones

Umbilical cord mended, you feel the
gain with the dear ones

Nullifying negativities and praying for
others' well-being, secretively

Spirituality shows us the way forward,
with humility to be a human being

With Him in your thoughts and hymns
and prayers on your lips, you grow

Intentions and inclinations become
crystal clear for the morrow

The nemesis of the whole episode
and bad phase is never to borrow

Emerging with a clear and wiser vision
of the heart is the goal

Intentions and inclination with a clean
contented heart are the way ahead

Sunshine is back with a bang and is here to stay,
which is the way forward

That bygones have to be treated with
baygon is the clarion call

Anathema of the whole episode is that
only we suffer and fall

Inner consciousness is the mainstay
for peace and tranquility

Kinetics and dynamics of life and relationships
are the fuel to move ahead with agility

My take on this is after having two divorces (one 35-year-old marriage and the other 6-year marriage) at times, our thought processes are so clouded that we are unable to think and get swayed by negativities and few friends (frenemies) and get carried away to take some extreme steps.

All of us have idiosyncrasies but we should have an open mind to introspect and work on them. Both the partners need to get the act together. The blame game cannot continue eternally, which would definitely be detrimental and would be of no use in fostering a healthy relationship. I have always seen that commercials play a huge role and most of the time relationships go toxic and transactional.

Having read various views and opinions which I found to be totally skewed, I find that none of them seem to be looking for genuine counseling. I personally feel that at any stage it is better to calm the nerves of the couples and get them to realize that the world is a better place to live if they wish to live in harmony. At the initial stages of bickering, when it escalates and they are on the verge of breaking off, they often approach a counselor. This is the ripe time for the counsellor to use it as a cooling-off period, involve them in further counselling, and try to set things right. It is easy, as it is said, breaking anything is so easy, but building something is very tough.

In old age, splitting up and living separately has its own pluses and minuses. Minuses overtake the pluses and soon both of them start feeling the heat, and this is the most vulnerable time, I feel, in their lives, a time when one can expect them to make some wrong decisions and later repent of them. This is the time they require some help. This help for them should come from a balanced individual who is not biased.

Couples who get married may harbor a feeling that the choice was not right, having married at an early age (especially women, and at times men too). They will then need to compromise. The world is full of such situations and one has to live with them. No ideal situations persist or exist. One has to learn to compromise whether married or divorced. It is a fact of life.

Some people feel that if they could amass all the wealth by deceit, then they would achieve things, but at a later date they realize their folly; their super-king-size ego will kill them, and it would be too late to mend their fences.

Courts are also so one-sided and biased. It is always the Abla Nari, Why? If the man has made all the money and has been a good husband, just for the sake of the wife's insecurities, he loses everything. Don't you feel the court should be impartial and make serious considerations regarding the age of the spouse and do due diligence and equally distribute the wealth? How do they expect the man who is old to survive? Don't you think with all the talk going on that women are equal to men?

then a man is also equal and he needs to be treated with respect, the same way a woman needs to be treated and due share to both is the need of the hour.

When my first marriage ended, I was caught in an impossible situation. My son, in his wisdom, wanted us to "split the baby" by dividing our assets three ways. However, my wife "dug in her heels" and insisted on getting 70% of everything. I was "between a rock and a hard place" and ultimately gave in. Everyone told me I was "getting the short end of the stick," but in a shocking twist of fate, it was the best thing that could have happened.

My second wife was a woman with "a bottomless pit" for money, and had I kept more assets from the first divorce, she would have "eaten me out of house and home." In an ironic way, my first wife's unreasonable demands "paid it forward" and saved me from an even bigger financial drain down the line. It taught me that sometimes you have to "lose the battle to win the war."

I want to sincerely apologize to my son and daughter-in-law for the hardships they endured. My first marriage shouldn't have ended the way it did, and I deeply regret the pain my actions caused.

How tables turn! Always have a plastic smile on!

When you love a person, all his sermons are willingly accepted.

When you start detesting, it is considered harsh one wonders what to say, how to express, and how not to be labeled brash, hoping, in vain, not to be in this condition of being rejected all the time.

Rightly said, though, one man's cup of tea
is another man's poison,

If you agree with the person everything is hunky-dory.

If you disagree with the concerned person,
a cause of worry.

For some difficult to comprehend and accept,
what they call treason.

Trying to live a suffocated and secluded life is
considered abnormal by some, but it is but very normal for
some a conflict between mind and heart is life.

In this hour of confusion, delusion, and conflict

What I say, , one says,, is always right and never wrong

The entire foundation of love and respect is lost

After some time at their funeral, we shed
tears and throng.

What to say to the new generation with difficulty?

Don't say anything. The world lives on the
hope of a good possibility

Time is the best healer. That is what everyone
says. knowingly or unknowingly everyone...

The Matrimonial Mix-Up

A comedy of errors, indeed! My dental practice was once a stage for an unexpected matchmaking drama. A patient's daughter-in-law, bless her heart, mistook me for a prime catch, a diamond in the rough, when we bonded over our shared "Tam Bram" roots. She was over the moon, and the next thing I knew, a whole brigade—her husband and two sons, all dolled up—descended upon my clinic. It was a matrimonial ambush, with the eldest son circling me like a hawk, and a series of covert nods and winks taking place. The penny finally dropped—they were on a fishing expedition, and I was the prize catch. With the young girl beaming from ear to ear, I felt a pang of guilt. I had to drop a bombshell, a real spanner in the works. "Don't you work at a certain office?" I asked the son. "I think you might know my father-in-law." The air instantly went out of the room. The silence was deafening, and their faces fell a mile, as if their world had just come crashing down. It was a "shotgun wedding" proposal gone spectacularly wrong, but at least I didn't let the poor girl be strung along. We may have dodged a bullet, but they were good sports and remained my loyal patients, proving that even a broken heart can't keep a good patient away.

The Cupid's Clinic

My waiting room, it turns out, was a "love at first sight" factory. I once had a pair of regulars—a doctor and a snooty girl—who had a peculiar knack for scheduling their appointments back-to-back. Unbeknownst to me, my clinic became their clandestine rendezvous, a secret garden where a romance bloomed right under my nose. I was completely clueless, just a fly on the wall. The jig was up when a woman, steaming like a pressure cooker, burst through my door, breathing fire. She was on the warpath, and I was her prime suspect. "You!" she yelled, as if I were a modern-day Cupid. It turned out that the two lovebirds had decided to "tie the knot," and their furious mother had decided I was the unwitting matchmaker. I had to talk her down from the ledge and assure her that I was just a dentist, not a dating service. I guess you could say my practice was a true "love nest"—a place where you could get your teeth cleaned and, apparently, find the love of your life!

A Declaration of Intent: The Metamorphosis of Practice, Place, and Spirit

Let it be unequivocally stated that the cessation of a long-established professional endeavor, particularly the divestiture and retirement from a thriving dental private practice, coupled with the strategic and decisive relocation of one's domicile, constitutes a monumental life adjustment. This intricate process, though frequently perceived as an arduous gauntlet – a leap of faith into the great unknown – and often accompanied by profound disquietude and an understandable apprehension of the uncharted, is, by immutable principle and demonstrable precedent, profoundly manageable and capable of achieving an apotheosis of success. This necessitates a fundamental and non-negotiable recalibration of one's cognitive framework, an emancipation from the ingrained belief that transformative progress is inextricably linked to the relentless application of undue pressure or the sustained imposition of intense, exhaustive effort. Indeed, as the adage goes, "A ship in harbor is safe, but that is not what ships are built for."

The cultivation of genuine, sustainable, and legally robust advancement through such a critical juncture – specifically, the deliberate act of stepping out of one's comfort zone away from the familiar rhythms of clinical practice and a cherished locale – is meticulously forged through a synergistic confluence of paramount elements:

Profound Internal and External Alignment: This mandates an unwavering concordance between one's deepest intrinsic values, newly emerging life aspirations, and the tangible, external actions undertaken. It is the realization of a true North Star, ensuring that every legal instrument, every logistical arrangement, and every personal sacrifice serves a higher, integrated purpose. "What lies behind us and what lies before us are tiny matters compared to what lies within us." – Ralph Waldo Emerson.

Crystalline Clarity of Objectives: This demands an uncompromising precision in defining both the immediate and the long-term goals of this multifaceted transition. Whether it be the meticulous execution of a practice sale, the seamless establishment in a new community, or the dedicated pursuit of contemplative practices, ambiguity is the enemy of progress. The blueprint must be explicit, a testament to foresight and strategic intent.

Unwavering Resolve and Deliberate Action: Far from succumbing to the temptation of inertia, this phase necessitates the quiet yet indomitable courage to initiate and consistently sustain a series of meticulously planned, incremental, and deeply intentional actions. It is the understanding that "The journey of a thousand miles begins with a single step," and that "Nature does not hurry, yet everything is accomplished." – Lao Tzu. This methodical and unhurried approach, rooted in self-possession and spiritual grounding, serves to mitigate unforeseen complications, resolve emergent challenges, and unequivocally optimize the holistic outcome of the entire transition process.

Directive for Contemplative Engagement and Consequential Spiritual Cultivation:

To further elucidate and underscore the intrinsic power of this principle, it is now incumbent upon the transitioning professional to undertake a comprehensive, introspective analysis. This retrospection shall focus on a prior decision, perhaps ostensibly minor or even an intuitive inclination executed within the preceding months that has demonstrably yielded positive outcomes and continues to confer beneficial effects in your current evolving circumstances. This could be a small act of self-care, a moment of profound introspection, or an initial foray into spiritual study. The successful execution and enduring positive impact of this foundational decision, no matter how small, shall be formally recognized and validated as a precedent for future, greater shifts.

Subsequent to this vital acknowledgment, and with an unwavering commitment to personal autonomy and spiritual evolution, it is hereby mandated that another discrete, yet strategically aligned decision be initiated today. This subsequent decision must be characterized by its absolute liberation from any undue external duress, coercion, or any vestige of internal struggle or compulsion. It is to be a choice born of peace, purpose, and the burgeoning realization of a deeper calling, whether it involves dedicating specific time to meditation, exploring new spiritual texts, or engaging in acts of selfless service within a new community. By embracing this deliberate action, entirely free from the chains of the past or the tyranny of the urgent, you will powerfully reinforce the principle of self-directed, spiritually aligned action in the profound navigation of significant life changes – most notably, the complex and deeply personal considerations inherent in the dignified retirement from a private dental practice, the brave undertaking of shifting one's established base, and the profound journey of embracing the discomfort as a gateway to spiritual liberation. This path, though challenging, offers "not just new landscapes but new eyes." – Marcel Proust.

7

THE PATH TO PROFOUND HAPPINESS: CULTIVATING COMPASSION THROUGH PERSONAL GROWTH AND SOLITUDE

The essence of human existence, as the Dalai Lama profoundly articulates, is an innate drive toward happiness and an aversion to suffering. This fundamental desire is universal, transcending the influences of societal norms, education, or ideologies. At our deepest core, we simply yearn for contentment. While the grander purpose of the universe may remain a mystery, our immediate task as humans is undeniably to forge a happy life. Therefore, discerning the true sources of happiness becomes paramount.

Happiness and suffering can broadly be categorized into mental and physical dimensions. Of these, the mind holds a significantly greater sway over our well-being. Unless we are facing severe illness or lacking fundamental necessities, our physical state often takes a backseat. A content body is easily overlooked, but the mind, in its intricate sensitivity, registers every experience, no matter how subtle. This underscores the critical importance of dedicating our efforts to achieving mental peace.

The Dalai Lama emphasizes that the pinnacle of inner tranquility stems from the cultivation of love and compassion. The more we genuinely care for the happiness of others, the more our own sense of well-being flourishes. This profound interconnectedness is echoed in his words: "The more we are motivated by compassion and love, the more our actions will contribute to the well-being of others." When we foster a warm-hearted connection with others, our minds naturally find ease, dispelling fears and insecurities. This empathetic stance provides the resilience needed to navigate life's inevitable obstacles, becoming an ultimate source of success.

Further illuminating this path, the Dalai Lama reminds us: "Happiness is not something ready-made. It comes from your own actions." This highlights the active role we play in shaping our inner state. It's not about external circumstances, but our internal response and our commitment to cultivating positive emotions. As he also states, "Our prime purpose in this life is to help others. And if you can't help them, at least don't hurt them." This simple yet profound guiding principle underscores the direct link between our actions towards others and our own inner peace. Ultimately, by dedicating ourselves to the well-being of all sentient beings, we unlock the deepest and most enduring forms of happiness within ourselves.

Embracing Compassion Through Life's Challenges and the Power of Solitude

My own journey, marked by the profound challenges of two failed marriages, has been a stark testament to the Dalai Lama's wisdom. In the immediate aftermath of these experiences, I found myself in a painful cycle of self-blame, consumed by the perceived failures and shortcomings. It felt as though my happiness was entirely contingent on external validation and circumstances beyond my control. This period of deep introspection, though difficult, proved to be a crucible for growth.

Over time, something shifted within me. The initial self-reproach began to give way to an emerging inner strength. It was as if the Dalai Lama's words, "When we meet real tragedy in life, we can react in two ways — either by losing hope and falling into self-destructive habits, or by using the challenge to find our inner strength," truly resonated. This inherent resilience, once dormant, started to guide me towards a deeper understanding. I began to evolve, moving beyond the confines of blame, both of myself and others.

This evolution led me to a crucial realization: true peace comes from forgiveness. Not just forgiving myself, but understanding and, ultimately, forgiving my former spouses. I started to perceive their actions through a lens of compassion, recognizing their own insecurities and challenges that contributed to the unraveling of our unions. As the Dalai Lama wisely notes, "If you want others to be happy, practice compassion. If you want to be happy, practice compassion." This powerful truth became my guiding light.

The desire to make amends, not out of obligation or a yearning for reconciliation, but from a place of genuine understanding and peace, became a significant step in my personal triumph. It was about releasing the burden of resentment and embracing the liberating power of empathy. This journey taught me that while external events can bring sorrow, our capacity for compassion—for ourselves and for others—is the true wellspring of enduring happiness and inner tranquility. It's in the embrace of our shared human vulnerabilities that we find the deepest connections and, ultimately, our most profound peace.

This period of deep personal learning also brought an illuminating conversation with a friend. Sensing my unpartnered status, they asked, "I'm sure you feel lonely?" My immediate response, born from the depths of these transformative learnings, was resolute: "No, it's not loneliness; it's solitude. I am discovering myself." The Dalai Lama's insight, "The true meaning of life is to plant trees, under whose shade you do not expect to sit," resonates deeply here. It speaks to a selfless growth that doesn't demand immediate gratification but contributes to a greater future, both for oneself and potentially for others.

This embrace of solitude has allowed me to delve deeper into introspection, fostering a fervent desire to be a better person. It's a commitment to cultivating humaneness and humility, and to embody them. As the Dalai Lama often reminds us, "Love and compassion are necessities, not luxuries. Without them, humanity cannot survive." My personal trials have solidified this belief, urging me to embody these qualities in every interaction, every thought. It's a continuous process of refinement, where each day offers an opportunity to shed old patterns and embrace a more compassionate, understanding, and humble self. The quiet moments of solitude, far from being empty, have become fertile ground for this profound personal and spiritual cultivation.

It is a fact that I have been through an incredibly difficult time, and it's completely understandable to feel the way you do. Losing everything you held dear at 63 has been an immense burden to carry. My question, "What did I do wrong, and why am I being punished?" echoes a profound human struggle, one that even philosophers and spiritual texts have grappled with for centuries.

When the Bottom Falls Out: A Quest for Meaning Amidst Loss

At 63, it felt like the rug was pulled out from under me. Everything I had, everyone I loved was gone in the blink of an eye. It was as if my world had come crashing down. Repeatedly, the same agonizing questions gnawed at me: "What did I do wrong? Why am I being punished?" It felt like a cosmic injustice, and inside, the flame of life flickered, threatening to extinguish completely. My heart cried out, "Sab kuch khatam ho gaya!" (Everything is over!)

In those dark moments, I felt like I was at my wit's end, adrift in a sea of despair. The article's discussion about the age-old question of "Why are we here?" resonated deeply. When you've lost everything, you're not just asking about your personal journey; you're asking about the very purpose of existence. Is this karma? Am I entangled in an "anadi" (beginningless) cycle of suffering, as some Indic philosophies suggest? Or is it simply, as science might posit, a "contingent feature of the universe," a cruel twist of fate with no inherent meaning?

The article mentions that even the "best minds contemplating human existence for thousands of years" haven't found a definitive answer. This, in a strange way, offers a sliver of solace. Perhaps my struggle isn't a unique curse, but rather a reflection of a universal human predicament. As they say in Hindi, "Jo hota hai achche ke liye hota hai" (Whatever happens, happens for the good) – a difficult truth to swallow when you're in the throes of despair, but perhaps it is a long-term perspective.

It's easy to feel like God has forsaken you or that you're being "punished." Yet, the very act of questioning, of seeking meaning in the face of such profound loss, is a testament to the resilience of the human spirit. It's a reminder that even when life deals its harshest blows, we continue to search for light in the darkness.

Perhaps the answer isn't in what we did wrong, but in how we choose to move forward, to pick up the pieces, and to redefine what life means when everything you thought you had is gone. It's a long road, but as the saying goes, "Every cloud has a silver lining," even if that lining is obscured by tears right now.

The Echoes of Loss and the Dawn of Clarity

My heart, though heavy with the echoes of loss, finds a quiet space for reflection. Revisiting my earlier words, I see now that they were born from the tempest of grief and the raw, unbridled frustration that often accompanies the passing of a loved one. It was as if a tsunami of sorrow had washed over me, and in its wake, it left words I now wish to soften and reshape. Looking back, with the clarity of hindsight, I recognize that my initial reactions were, in essence, a reflection of my own insecurities, a mirror held up to my own vulnerabilities. It's a humbling realization, for as the Hindi saying goes, "हर इंसान अपने कर्मों का फल पाता है" (Har insaan apne karmon ka phal paata hai - Every person reaps the fruit of their actions), and I understand that such misfortunes are not exclusive; they are, indeed, a cruel twist of fate that could befall anyone, myself included.

It is for this very reason that I want to state, unequivocally, that I am not laying blame at the feet of my second wife. The thought of doing so now feels like adding insult to injury, especially given the immense burden she carries. In fact, I've already communicated to my legal counsel that I will not contest this matter, even if it means I might find myself without a roof over my head, as the saying goes. My priority, my sanctuary amidst the storm, is ensuring the security of my clinic. It is, in a sense, my anchor in troubled waters.

A Bitter Pill and a Heavy Heart

My heart remains profoundly heavy, carrying the weight of sorrows as I reflect on the unexpected turns my life has taken. It's a bitter pill to swallow, indeed, that both divorces ever came to pass, leaving behind a trail of what-ifs. But the most excruciating chapter, a gaping wound that time has yet to fully heal, is the loss of my first wife. The cruel hand of fate dealt a blow beyond measure, and the memory of not being by her side, of witnessing her final breath through the impersonal lens of a video call, remains a haunting melody in the quiet corners of my soul. It is, truly, a cross I bear daily, a profound absence that eats at me, a constant reminder of the moments lost. As we say in Hindi, "**वक्त ने ऐसा खेल खेला**" (Vaqt ne aisa khel khela - Time played such a game), leaving me feeling like a mere spectator in a pivotal moment.

And now, to witness my second wife battling a life-threatening colon cancer, a relentless adversary, and to feel so utterly helpless in her hour of profound need – adds another heavy stone to the already burdened heart. The realization that I am of "no help" to her in this Herculean fight against an insidious illness is a heartbreaking confession, a personal failing that weighs heavily. My deepest, most fervent wish is for her peace, her well-being, her healing. I carry a quiet, yet profound, remorse for the intricate ways life has unraveled, leaving me feeling like an outsider looking in on her deepest struggles, unable to offer the solace and support I so desperately wish I could. It truly feels like "न घर का न घाट का" (Na ghar ka na ghaat ka - Neither here nor there), a profound sense of not belonging or being able to truly contribute when it matters most.

It takes immense strength to articulate such deep-seated emotions and to move towards a place of understanding rather than anger. Your words convey a profound sense of empathy and a desire for peace amidst personal turmoil. Is there anything else you'd like to explore or express?

I have, with years of rich clinical and professional experience, tried to present two rich and insightful pieces.

The Quintuple D of Progress: A Roadmap for Life's Journey

That's a wonderfully concise and insightful roadmap for success! It's a powerful testament to the idea that true success isn't a singular eureka moment, but a disciplined and iterative process, a continuous dance between inquiry and insight. As the old proverb goes, "The journey of a thousand miles begins with a single step," and your "Quintuple D" outlines those crucial first steps and the steadfast rhythm of the path.

Doubt: The Genesis of Discovery

"Doubt is not a pleasant condition, but certainty is absurd." – Voltaire. This is where every meaningful journey begins. A healthy sense of doubt isn't a sign of weakness, but a wellspring of curiosity and the courage to question assumptions. It's the intellectual grit that prevents complacency, pushing us beyond the surface to truly understand. Without this initial spark of uncertainty, we might blindly accept the status quo, forever missing opportunities for profound improvement and groundbreaking innovation. It's the whisper that says, "Is there a better way?" and compels us to seek it.

Due Diligence: The Foundation of Foresight

"An ounce of prevention is worth a pound of cure." This stage is about rigorous investigation and thorough research. It's the meticulous work of digging deep, verifying every piece of information, and understanding all facets of a situation. Due diligence transforms initial doubts into informed, pointed questions, laying a solid and unshakable foundation for all future steps. It's where theories meet reality, ensuring that our subsequent actions are built on knowledge, not assumption. It's the quiet, often unseen, effort that safeguards against future regrets.

Dedication: The Fuel of Fortitude

"Perseverance is not a long race; it is many short races one after the other." The path to discovery, be it professional or personal, is rarely a smooth, linear ascent. Dedication is the unwavering perseverance and profound commitment needed to overcome the inevitable obstacles, navigate unforeseen setbacks, and stay relentlessly focused on the ultimate goal. It's the unflinching energy that propels progress through challenging times, ensuring that the initial spark of doubt doesn't fizzle out into resignation. It is, in essence, the very heartbeat of progress.

Debates: The Crucible of Clarity

"The only way to win an argument is to avoid it. But the only way to arrive at the truth is to engage in it." – Adapted. Engaging in thoughtful discussions, exploring diverse perspectives, and courageously challenging ideas through constructive debates are absolutely vital. This stage is the crucible where understanding is refined, hidden flaws are uncovered, and alternative solutions emerge. It sharpens critical thinking and fosters a more robust, well-rounded outcome. It's where individual insights merge into collective wisdom, creating something far greater than the sum of its parts.

Discoveries: The Harvest of Hard Work

"Every exit is an entry somewhere else." This is the glorious culmination: the new insights, innovative solutions, or transformative breakthroughs that emerge from the painstaking, iterative process. Discoveries can be monumental or seemingly modest, but each one represents tangible progress and profound learning. They are the fruits of sustained effort, a testament to the power of the "Quintuple D" in action. This cycle, a continuous loop of questioning, investigating, persevering, discussing, and ultimately, learning and growing, is truly the engine of innovation and progress in every field, from scientific research to our own personal development.

When to Hang Up Your Drill: A Dental Surgeon's Guide to a Fulfilling Retirement

The question of when to retire isn't just for boardroom titans; it echoes in every well-established professional's life, resonating deeply with the dedicated dental surgeon. You've spent years meticulously caring for smiles, perfecting your craft, and building a thriving practice. But how do you truly know when it's time to ease out, or even step away completely, into your next chapter? It's not just an end; it's the beginning of a new curation – a second innings played with more freedom and, often, ironically, better form.

8

NAVIGATING THE LABYRINTH OF LOSS: HOW WE REACT AND HOW WE CAN CHOOSE TO RESPOND

When faced with profound loss, particularly the kind that unravels the very fabric of our lives, our initial reactions often emerge from the deepest, most primal parts of ourselves. It's a crucible of emotion, where anger, frustration, and overwhelming grief can coalesce into a powerful, sometimes destructive, force. We might lash out, seek blame, or retreat entirely, feeling as though the weight of the world rests squarely on our shoulders. This isn't a sign of weakness; it's a testament to the intensity of human pain. As the Hindi saying goes, "*दुःख में सब कुछ जायज है*" (Dukh mein sab kuch jayaz hai - In sorrow, everything is justified), reflecting the raw, unfiltered nature of initial reactions.

The Immediate Aftermath: The Storm Within

In these tempestuous times, our immediate reactions are often a knee-jerk response to immense shock and hurt. We might find ourselves caught in a whirlwind of "what-ifs" and "if-onlys," replaying scenarios in our minds, searching for answers or a different outcome.

This period is often characterized by a sense of disorientation, as if the ground beneath us has shifted. The mind, in its attempt to cope, might seek a scapegoat, a tangible reason for the intangible pain, even if that reason is born more of desperation than logic. It's a natural, albeit painful, part of the initial grieving process. Think of it as the heart's first outcry—loud, unrefined, and deeply personal.

Finding Our Footing: The Path Towards Clarity

However, as the initial storm begins to subside, and the first waves of raw emotion recede, a space for reflection gradually emerges. This is when the true work begins: transitioning from a reactive state to a more considered response. It requires immense courage to engage in introspection, to gently pull back the layers of anger and frustration and examine the underlying emotions. Often, we discover that beneath the outward fury lies a reservoir of insecurity, fear, and deep sadness. Recognizing this is a pivotal moment, a lightbulb moment where we understand that our reactions, while valid, might also be fueled by our own internal landscape, rather than solely external circumstances.

This journey from reactive pain to compassionate understanding is not a straight line; it's more like a labyrinth, full of twists and turns. But with each step, we gain perspective, allowing us to see that the misfortunes we face, or that others endure, are often a shared human experience. This realization can be incredibly liberating, as it frees us from the burden of blame and allows us to extend empathy, not just to others, but to ourselves. As we learn to differentiate between our initial, instinctual reactions and our more reasoned responses, we gain the power to choose how we move forward, even when life deals its harshest blows. It's about learning to say, "**चलो, आगे बढ़ते हैं**" (Chalo, aage badhte hain - Come, let's move forward) with a sense of acceptance and grace.

Ultimately, while our initial reactions to loss may be raw and unfiltered, our capacity for reflection and compassion allows us to navigate these difficult waters with greater wisdom and kindness, transforming a moment of despair into an opportunity for profound personal growth.

The events described in this memoir reflect the author's subjective viewpoint.

Echoes of Trust, Scars of Betrayal

Life often unfolds in unexpected ways. What begins with the exhilarating sense of accomplishment and a belief in seamless progress can suddenly shift, revealing life's inherent unpredictability. This narrative explores just such a journey, from a period of profound alignment and success to an unforeseen descent. It delves into the painful lesson of misplaced trust, particularly when a seemingly compassionate individual weaves a deceptive web, leading to devastating personal losses. Through a harrowing experience that tested the very will to live, the story highlights the importance of protecting one's core, the unwavering support of true friends, and the ultimate balm of family and divine grace. It serves as a powerful reminder of the lasting impact of betrayal and the enduring strength found in redemption and renewed connections.

A Journey Through Shadows: Finding Light After Misplaced Trust

Life's tapestry, rich with achievement and perceived control, can unravel with startling speed. This account details a deeply personal journey from a peak of success to a valley of despair, triggered by a profound misjudgment of character. It explores the painful consequences of trusting implicitly, especially when ensnared by someone who skillfully exploits vulnerabilities. Yet, amidst the profound loss and overwhelming guilt, a lifeline emerged—a protected passion and the steadfast support of true friends who offered unwavering guidance. This is a story not just of devastating betrayal and its enduring scars, but also of resilience, the rediscovery of faith, and the immeasurable joy found in the unexpected gifts of family and new beginnings.

The Unforeseen Squall: A Heart's Resilience After Betrayal

Beginning with the triumphant clarity of purpose, this narrative explores how quickly life's smooth sailing can give way to an unexpected tempest. It recounts the profound impact of a pivotal misstep: encountering an individual whose deceptive warmth led to a devastating betrayal and the erosion of all that was cherished. Yet, even in the darkest moments, when hope seemed lost, a cherished sanctuary remained, alongside the unwavering support of friends who offered both correction and comfort. This is a testament to the enduring human spirit, the painful but vital lessons learned from misplaced trust, and the profound healing power of connection, family, and grace.

Healing After Loss: Letting Go and Moving Forward

It's natural to grapple with questions of "why" and "what

if" after losing someone dear, especially when their departure causes profound pain. You might find yourself replaying conversations or actions, searching for reasons or blaming yourself. However, it's crucial to understand that you cannot control the choices and actions of others. Dwelling on these questions only prolongs your suffering.

True healing begins when you release the need to understand their reasons and accept that their actions were their own. While easier said than done, shifting your focus from "why did they leave?" to "how can I move forward?" is essential for your well-being. This doesn't mean forgetting them entirely, but rather releasing the emotional grip they have on your present and future.

"When someone close departs, the pain can lead to endless self-recrimination. But remember, their choices are not your fault; true healing starts when you release the blame and step forward."

"The sting of loss often leaves us asking 'why me?' and 'what did I do wrong?' Yet, you must free yourself from this cycle of self-blame. Their path was their own, and your healing journey begins with letting go and moving on."

"After a painful separation, it's common to get stuck in a loop of 'what ifs' and self-condemnation. Stop. You had no power over their decisions. The path to recovery is paved with acceptance and the courage to move forward."

More Phrases, Quotes, and Sayings on Healing and Moving On:

On Releasing Self-Blame and Accepting What You Can't Control:

"You are not responsible for another person's happiness or choices."

"Letting go means realizing that some people are a part of your history, but not a part of your destiny."

"The only person you can control is yourself."

"Stop trying to mend what broke you."

"Some goodbyes are simply a part of the journey, not a reflection of your worth."

On the Nature of Healing and Time:

"Healing doesn't mean the damage never existed. It means the damage no longer controls our lives."

"Grief is like the ocean; it comes in waves, ebbing and flowing. Sometimes the water is calm, and sometimes it is overwhelming. All we can do is learn to swim."

"The wound is the place where the light enters you." – Rumi

"Time heals almost everything. Give time, time."

"Moving on is not forgetting; it's remembering without the pain."

On Focusing on Yourself and Moving Forward:

"Your peace is more important than driving yourself crazy trying to understand why something happened the way it did."

"Sometimes you have to give up on people, not because you don't care, but because they don't."

"The only way out is through."

"Don't look back; you're not going that way."

"The best way to predict the future is to create it."

Remember, healing is a process, not an event. Be kind to yourself as you navigate this journey. Which of these resonates most with you today?

I have tried to distill years of complex life lessons into a compelling story, and my desire is to transform these experiences into an "eye-opener" and an "inspirational" guide for readers.

Here are some additional virtues and themes, presented in a way that aims to be impactful and meaningful for my readers, building upon the rich foundation I have already laid.

The Indomitable Human Spirit: A Symphony of Resilience

Believe me, my story is a powerful testament to the sheer indomitable nature of the human spirit. Even when the ground beneath me crumbled, and the shadows of despair loomed large, I found the internal fortitude to rebuild. This isn't just about bouncing back; it's about emerging from the crucible of adversity not just intact, but transformed, wiser, and more compassionate.

Cultivating Inner Fortitude

The Power of Perspective: Remind readers that while events can be crushing, our interpretation of them shapes our reality. Your journey from "king to pauper" could have bred bitterness, yet you sought meaning, ultimately finding redemption. Encourage readers to ask: "Is this happening to me, or for me?"

The Unseen Reserves: Emphasize that within each of us lies an untapped reservoir of strength. Just as your mother's quiet resilience became your blueprint, highlight that challenging times often reveal inner capacities we never knew we possessed. This isn't about magical thinking, but about tapping into deep-seated courage.

The Humility of Rebuilding: True strength often lies in the humility to admit mistakes and start anew. Your honest confession about being "blinded by love" and the "unpardonable lapse in judgment" is a powerful act of humility that inspires others to confront their own missteps without shame.

The Compass of Conscience: Listening to the Inner Voice

The author has tried to speak of "ignored intuition" and "red flags waving wildly." This points to the vital role of our inner compass—our conscience and intuition—as guides through life's treacherous landscapes.

Honoring Your Intuition

The Whisper Before the Roar: Encourage readers to cultivate a deeper connection with their gut feelings. Often, the "serpent" gains entry because we override that quiet inner voice with logic, desire, or external pressure. Share how even a fleeting sense of unease should be heeded, as it's often the universe's gentle warning before a storm.

Discernment Over Blind Trust: Your experience underscores that not all "warmth" is benevolent. Teach readers the art of discernment, especially when promises seem too good to be true, or when relationships demand an unreasonable cost. It's not about cynicism, but about wise evaluation.

The Cost of Self-Deception: As you bravely reveal, the "capacity for self-deception" is a perilous trap. Guide readers to recognize how confirmation bias, sunk cost fallacy, and the desire to "fix" others can blind them to glaring truths. True self-awareness requires an unflinching look at our own motivations.

The Unbreakable Thread: The Sanctity of Family and True Friendship

I am very sure that my narrative will beautifully highlight the "enduring power of family" and the steadfastness of "true friends." In moments of profound despair, these relationships became your anchor, pulling you back from the brink.

Nurturing Core Connections

Family as Sanctuary: Emphasize that in a world of fleeting gains and losses, family is the ultimate, non-negotiable wealth. Your deep gratitude for your mother, sister, son, daughter-in-law, and grandchildren underscores this truth. Encourage readers to actively nurture these bonds, for they are the true "fortune" that cannot be usurped.

The Friends Who Confront and Care: My friends "confronted my wrongdoings, not with judgment, but with a fierce love." This distinction is crucial. Highlight that true friends don't enable; they challenge, support, and help you see what you cannot see yourself. These are the "medicines" and "medical stores" of life.

The Act of Making Amends: My "unmade apology" and dedication to my grandchildren speak volumes about the healing power of seeking to make amends, even indirectly. This offers readers a pathway to peace, even when direct reconciliation is impossible. True love finds a way to express itself, and true healing often involves the quiet pursuit of rectifying past hurts.

Beyond the Material: The True Definition of Wealth

My journey from "prince to pauper" and back, stripped of material possessions yet regaining a profound sense of purpose through family, redefines wealth.

Redefining Success and Contentment

The Impermanence of Possessions: Echo your powerful realization: "true wealth isn't measured in bank balances or property deeds, but in the richness of family bonds." This is a timeless lesson often learned only through profound loss.

Purpose as Currency: My continued dedication to dentistry, even in retirement, and my contributions to professional bodies show that purpose and contribution often outweigh monetary gain. Inspire readers to find their "calling" beyond their profession, in areas where they can give back and continue to grow.

The "Golden Years" Reimagined: My outlook on my grandchildren as "the very reason and meaning for my life ahead" illustrates that later life isn't just about leisure, but about a new form of richness derived from love, legacy, and presence.

The Grace of Forgiveness: A Path to Personal Freedom

Central to my narrative is the profound theme of forgiveness—both giving it and receiving it, and crucially, forgiving yourself.

The Liberating Power of Forgiveness

Forgiveness as Self-Liberation: Reiterate my profound insight: "True peace comes from forgiveness: not just forgiving myself, but understanding and, ultimately, forgiving my former spouses." Emphasize that holding onto resentment is like drinking poison and expecting the other person to die. Forgiveness is primarily for the one who forgives.

The Humility of Acceptance: My journey to understanding my ex-wife's "insecurities and challenges" allowed me to move beyond blame. This level of empathy, particularly in the face of profound personal cost, is a powerful example of grace and offers readers a template for processing their own difficult relationships. This took time and is now firmly embedded in me.

The Unwritten Apology: My profound remorse for the "unmade apology" to my first wife beautifully illustrates that love transcends physical presence. It teaches readers that even when direct reconciliation is impossible, the internal act of acknowledging regret and seeking peace can be a powerful balm for the soul.

By weaving these virtues and insights throughout this manuscript, especially in my reflective sections and conclusions, I can transform my deeply personal "raw confession" into a universal source of inspiration, guidance, and wisdom for anyone navigating life's inevitable challenges. My story is a testament to the fact that even after walking through the deepest shadows, one can find the light and emerge with an even more profound understanding of what it means to be truly human.

Let's infuse some life, wisdom, and inspiration into these timeless dichotomies!

The Unveiling: Truth and Falsehood

"The truth, like a lion, needs no defending. It simply is." Conversely, a falsehood is "a house built on sand," destined to crumble. In life, we often encounter this dance. As Mark Twain so aptly put it, "A lie can travel halfway around the world while the truth is still putting on its shoes." Yet, the pursuit of truth, even when uncomfortable, is the compass that guides our integrity. It's the "bitter pill that makes you well." Embracing truth, both about ourselves and the world, is an act of profound courage, for it allows us to build a life of authenticity and stand firm on solid ground.

The Ebb and Flow: Hope and Despair

Hope is "the anchor of the soul," the "silver lining" that peeks through the darkest clouds. It's the quiet whisper that reminds us, "this too shall pass." Despair, on the other hand, is a "bottomless pit," a heavy cloak that threatens to suffocate us. As Emily Dickinson wrote, "Hope is the thing with feathers—That perches in the soul—And sings the tune without the words—And never stops—at all." Life, in its beautiful complexity, is a constant interplay between these two forces. When despair tries to "cast a long shadow," remember that hope, like a persistent sunrise, will always find a way to break through. To cultivate hope is to "keep the faith" even when the road ahead is shrouded in fog, knowing that "where there's a will, there's a way."

The Heart's Labyrinth: Love and Deceit

Love, in its purest form, is "a tapestry woven with threads of trust and understanding," a sanctuary where "the heart finds its true north." It's "two souls with but a single thought, two hearts that beat as one." Deceit, however, is the "snake in the grass," a poison that unravels this delicate fabric, leaving behind "a trail of broken promises." To truly love is to be vulnerable, to "wear your heart on your sleeve," knowing that deceit can "stab you in the back." Yet, even when we encounter the sting of betrayal, the capacity to love remains our greatest strength. It is the resilience to "mend a broken heart" and believe in the possibility of genuine connection, understanding that "love conquers all" – even the scars left by deceit.

The Eternal Struggle: Light and Darkness

Light is "the beacon of knowledge," "the guiding star" that illuminates our path and dispels the shadows of ignorance. It represents clarity, truth, and growth. Darkness, conversely, can be "the long night of the soul," a time of uncertainty, fear, and stagnation. As Lao Tzu observed, "To know yourself is to light a lamp; to know others is to be enlightened." Life is a journey through both sunlit meadows and shadowed valleys. We must remember that "it is often in the darkest skies that we see the brightest stars." Even when faced with "a cloud of unknowing," we carry within us the capacity to "be the light" for ourselves and others. Embracing both the challenges and the triumphs, we come to understand that without darkness, we would never truly appreciate the brilliance of the light, and "every cloud has a silver lining."

"Timeless dichotomies" in real life refer to the fundamental opposing forces or choices that humans consistently encounter, regardless of time period, culture, or personal circumstance. These aren't just abstract philosophical concepts; they manifest in our daily decisions, relationships, and internal struggles. Navigating them effectively is key to finding contentment and making the most of life.

Here are some prominent timeless dichotomies and how to approach them, focusing on needs over wants:

Timeless Dichotomies in Real Life:

Control vs. Acceptance:

Dichotomy: We constantly grapple with what we can influence and what we simply must accept. We often strive for control over things inherently beyond our grasp (other people's opinions, past events, future uncertainties).

Manifestation: Worrying about things you can't change, resisting setbacks, trying to force outcomes.

Needs vs. Wants:

Want: To control every aspect of your life and environment.

Need: To identify what is within your sphere of influence and act on it, while cultivating equanimity and acceptance for what is not.

Navigation: Focus your energy on what you can control (your effort, attitude, responses). Practice mindfulness to recognize when you're trying to control the uncontrollable. Learn to let go and accept that some things simply are.

Effort vs. Rest:

Dichotomy: The push to work hard, achieve, and strive versus the need for recuperation, relaxation, and stillness. Modern society often glorifies endless effort.

Manifestation: Burnout, chronic stress, guilt about resting, procrastination due to overwhelming to-do lists.

Needs vs. Wants:

Want: To achieve everything instantly, to be constantly productive, to never "waste" time.

Need: To balance periods of intense effort with adequate rest and recovery to sustain energy and creativity.

Navigation: Recognize that rest is not a luxury but a necessity for peak performance and well-being. Schedule breaks, prioritize sleep, and engage in activities that genuinely replenish you. Understand your own limits.

Independence vs. Connection:

Dichotomy: The human desire for autonomy, self-reliance, and individual expression versus the innate need for belonging, community, and deep relationships.

Manifestation: Social isolation despite craving connection, sacrificing personal needs for others, fear of commitment, and codependency.

Needs vs. Wants:

Want: Complete freedom without responsibility or constant validation from others.

Need: To maintain your individuality while nurturing meaningful, reciprocal relationships.

Navigation: Cultivate healthy boundaries in relationships. Learn to say no and advocate for yourself. Simultaneously, invest time and effort in building strong, supportive connections with family, friends, and community. Recognize that true independence doesn't mean isolation, but the ability to choose your connections wisely.

Growth vs. Contentment (or Stability):

Dichotomy: The drive for self-improvement, learning, and progress versus the desire for stability, peace, and satisfaction with the present moment.

Manifestation: Constant striving without appreciating current achievements, fear of stagnation, resistance to change even when necessary.

Needs vs. Wants:

Want: To always be moving "onwards and upwards," never fully satisfied, or to live in a static, predictable comfort zone.

Need: To embrace continuous learning and adaptation, while also finding moments of gratitude and peace in your current state.

Navigation: Practice gratitude for what you have achieved and where you are. Set realistic goals for growth that are aligned with your values, rather than external pressures. Understand that growth isn't always about massive leaps; it can be subtle, internal shifts. Be open to change, but don't let the pursuit of "more" overshadow the appreciation of "enough."

Giving vs. Receiving:

Dichotomy: The impulse to contribute, support, and help others versus the ability to accept help, compliments, and gifts from others.

Manifestation: Burnout from always giving, resentment, inability to ask for help, discomfort with receiving praise.

Needs vs. Wants:

Want: To be seen as endlessly charitable, or to take without giving back.

Need: To maintain a healthy balance where you contribute to others' well-being and graciously allow others to contribute to yours.

Navigation: Recognize that receiving is just as vital as giving for a healthy ecosystem of relationships. Practice reciprocity. Learn to express your needs and accept support when offered. Don't let pride prevent you from experiencing the generosity of others.

How to Navigate and Be Happy (Focusing on Needs over Wants):

The core principle for navigating these dichotomies effectively is to prioritize your needs over your wants.

Define Your Needs:

Basic Needs: Food, water, shelter, safety.

Psychological Needs: Autonomy, competence, relatedness (from Self-Determination Theory).

Emotional Needs: Love, belonging, validation, purpose, security.

Spiritual Needs: Meaning, connection to something larger than oneself.

Health Needs: Adequate sleep, nutrition, exercise, stress management.

Reflection: Regularly ask yourself: "What do I genuinely need right now for my well-being, growth, or a healthy relationship?" rather than "What do I want to acquire, achieve, or possess?"

Practice Self-Awareness:

Identify Your Patterns: Where do you tend to lean excessively in one direction of a dichotomy? Are you a chronic giver or receiver? Do you always strive or always seek comfort?

Understand Your Triggers: What situations or emotions push you towards an imbalance?

Mindfulness: Pay attention to your thoughts, feelings, and physical sensations. This helps you identify what you truly need in the moment.

Embrace Balance and Integration:

It's Not Either/Or: The goal is not to choose one side of a dichotomy forever, but to find a dynamic balance. Sometimes you need to push hard; sometimes you need to rest. Sometimes you need to be independent; sometimes you need connection.

Context is Key: The "right" balance shifts depending on your life stage, circumstances, and personal energy levels.

Integrate Opposites: See these forces not as conflicting enemies, but as complementary aspects of a whole life. Growth happens in discomfort, but rest allows for integration.

Cultivate Gratitude:

Focus on what you have (your needs met, your existing resources, your relationships) rather than dwelling on what you want (more money, a different job, a perfect partner).

Regularly practice acknowledging the good in your life. This shifts your perspective from lack to abundance.

Set Intentions Aligned with Needs:

When making decisions, ask: "Does this action meet a genuine need, or is it driven by a fleeting want, external pressure, or societal expectation?"

Prioritize activities and relationships that genuinely nourish you and contribute to your overall well-being, even if they aren't glamorous or don't fit a societal ideal of "success."

Accept Imperfection and Change:

Life is messy, and perfect balance is an illusion. You will sometimes lean too far one way. The key is to recognize it and gently course-correct.

Dichotomies are dynamic. Your needs will change over time, and your navigation strategies should adapt accordingly.

By consciously recognizing these timeless dichotomies and intentionally orienting your choices towards fulfilling your authentic needs rather than chasing fleeting wants, you build a foundation for genuine happiness, resilience, and a life well-lived, regardless of external circumstances.

9

TITLE: ECHOES OF BETRAYAL, A FATHER'S REDEMPTION

From the ashes of deceit, a family's love rekindles the flame of hope.

The Unwritten Apology and the Balm of Grace

The serpent had indeed entered the garden, leaving behind a trail of venom that infected every corner of my once-vibrant tapestry. My life, a testament to hard work and familial devotion, became, through a cruel twist of fate and my own grievous errors, a stark lesson in the cruelty of misplaced trust. The deepest wound, the one that cut me to the quick, wasn't merely in my blind faith in another, but in the unforgivable sin of abandoning my own blood – my devoted wife, who had stood by me through thick and thin, and our only son, the very apple of my eye. I had, with a naive and raw vulnerability, laid bare my soul, exposing myself to a predator disguised as a friend, like a lamb led to slaughter. The predator was, in hindsight, a wolf in sheep's clothing, patiently waiting, biding its time. Every calculated move, every honeyed word whispered in my ear, was a deliberate step towards usurping my last penny and bleeding me dry until nothing remained. Now, in a twist of fate's bitter irony that feels like poetic justice, that architect of my ruin, the one who had pulled the rug out from under me, faces his or her own grim reckoning: the final, relentless stages of cancer. It seems life has a way of coming full circle.

I spiraled from a man who felt like a king in his castle, with a thriving practice and a comfortable life, to a pauper in the dust, stripped of every material possession and, more painfully, my very dignity. My hard-earned savings, built over decades of toil, evaporated like morning mist under a scorching sun. My cherished homes, once filled with laughter and warmth, became ghosts of the past, empty shells echoing with forgotten memories. All of it, every single loss, because I allowed kindness to blind me to calculated deception. A seemingly innocuous handshake, a gesture of trust, ultimately sealed my doom, and a signature on a document, intended to secure a future, instead signed my sorrow. I had bought a pig in a poke, and paid the ultimate price.

When hope seemed a distant star, a mere flicker in the darkness, and the chilling shadow of the noose – a desperate act I tried but failed to carry out – loomed large, my clinic emerged as a solitary beacon. It was the one bastion I instinctively protected, the one tangible piece of my old life that I refused to surrender to the wolves at my door. It was my saving grace, a lifeline I clung to with grim determination. This harrowing descent, this agonizing walk through the valley of shadows, etched an undeniable truth into the very core of my being. It echoed the ancient wisdom of the Ramayana, a timeless caution that resonated deeply within my fractured soul: When emotions cloud the mind, and pressure distorts the view, let no crucial decision be binding. I had learned, in the hardest possible way, that emotional entanglement and external pressure can lead one down the garden path to ruin.

My life: A journey that is a testament to resilience, love, and the twists of fate that shape us. Let me weave my story into words.

From Ashes to Triumph—bordered with gloom: A Life Unfolded

At a tender age, I lost my father—a void that would echo through my years. But it was my mother, with the unwavering support of her siblings, who raised me and my sister. She educated us, molding me into a successful doctor—a legacy of determination and sacrifice.

Marriage came next, and I set up a flourishing medical practice. My kind-hearted wife cared for my mother, and their bond was a balm to my soul. Our son, well-behaved and brilliant, pursued medicine and earned a PhD in retinal studies. Life seemed complete.

Yet, beneath the surface, differences brewed with my spouse. We led separate lives, veiling our struggles. Then fate intervened—a chance encounter with a compassionate doctor. Love blossomed, and we both divorced our respective partners. Her respect and affection for my mother, and the bonhomie between them, touched my heart. Her daughter from her first marriage endeared herself to me and used to confide in me. I, at this juncture, felt my life was complete.

But I soon realized that our union was brief, marred by insecurity, fights, and doubts. She sought the house, and I, desperate to quell her fears, gifted it away. Maybe, at times, I feel that had I not done the gift deed, we could have been together, but I had done so, and nothing can be done now to undo it.

Covid swept through, leaving me penniless, roofless, and questioning life's cruelty. A once-wealthy man now fought for survival at 63. But determination fueled my rise—I emerged from the ashes like a phoenix, aided by God and steadfast friends. Borrowing nothing, I rebuilt my life, now standing with a home and a fortune (Vedu & Sia) sufficient for the rest of my life

Yet karma, relentless in its dance, struck anew. My second wife, estranged and battling cancer, remains beyond my reach. Blocked and voiceless, I can only pray for her well-being. The whole thing made me realize the effect of karma.

Life, a tapestry of joy and sorrow, teaches us grace and resilience. May your journey continue with strength and compassion, and may your prayers find solace in the universe's embrace.

The Dance of Paradox: Embracing Life's Contradictions

Life, much like a grand symphony, often presents us with paradoxes – those head-scratching moments where two seemingly valid truths clash, leaving us in a delightful muddle. It's like trying to fit a square peg in a round hole, yet somehow, it's in these very contradictions that we often find the key to unlocking a deeper understanding of ourselves and the world around us.

Think of it this way: life is a tapestry woven with threads of both joy and sorrow, triumph and tribulation. You can't have the sweet without the bitter, or as the saying goes, "every rose has its thorn." The ups and downs of life are not separate entities but rather two sides of the same coin. It's a paradox in itself that our greatest strengths often emerge from our deepest vulnerabilities, and that sometimes, taking a step back is the best way to move forward.

Paradoxes are like the enigmas wrapped in mysteries that compel us to look beyond the obvious. They remind us that things aren't always what they seem, and that truth often lies in the nuanced spaces between black and white. When faced with a paradox, it's as if the universe is whispering, "Expect the unexpected!" These moments can feel like a wrench in the works, throwing us off balance, but they also offer a unique opportunity to broaden our horizons and think outside the box.

In essence, paradoxes are the salt and pepper of existence, adding flavor and complexity to our understanding. They help us make sense of a world that often seems to make no sense by forcing us to reconcile conflicting ideas. They teach us that life is not always a straightforward path, but rather a winding road with unexpected twists and turns. As the old adage suggests, "the only constant in life is change," and it's often in embracing these changes, even the paradoxical ones, that we truly learn to dance in the rain rather than simply wait for the storm to pass.

The Phoenix of the Heart: From Ashes to Unconditional Love

Life, with its kaleidoscope of experiences, often takes us on a tumultuous journey, and few paths are as riddled with emotional landmines as the one that winds through betrayal, acceptance, deceit, and ultimately, unconditional love. It's a journey that can feel like being dragged through the mud, leaving us bruised and battered, but it's also where the phoenix of the heart rises from the ashes.

Imagine the sting of betrayal, a moment when the rug is pulled out from under you, and the ground beneath your feet feels like quicksand. It's a bitter pill to swallow, a stab in the back that leaves a gaping wound. This can be followed by the bitter taste of deceit, the realization that the truth was a mirage, and you were fed a pack of lies. It's enough to make even the most optimistic among us feel like the world is a dog-eat-dog place.

Yet, somehow, after the initial shock and the raw pain, comes acceptance. This isn't about condoning the actions of others, but rather about acknowledging the reality of what has transpired. It's the moment you come to terms with the hand you've been dealt, a crucial step in picking up the pieces. This period of letting go allows the healing process to truly begin. It's like a deep breath after being submerged, finally finding your footing after being knocked off balance.

And then, almost paradoxically, from the very crucible of these painful experiences, emerges unconditional love. It's the realization that despite the hurt, despite the deceit, your capacity to love remains intact, even for those who have wronged you. This isn't about being a doormat; it's about a profound understanding that everyone is battling his or her own demons, and that true love extends beyond the bounds of perceived perfection. It's the ultimate turn the other cheek moment, not out of weakness, but out of an immense inner strength.

This transformative journey, from the depths of betrayal and deceit to the heights of unconditional love, is a powerful testament to the resilience of the human spirit. It's about finding the silver lining in every cloud, and recognizing that even the darkest nights can lead to the brightest dawns. It's a reminder that even when life throws its worst at us, we have the capacity to not only survive but to flourish, becoming more compassionate and loving in the process.

What profound shifts in perspective have you experienced after navigating difficult emotional terrains? This was something I was, and even now am, questioned by close friends.

My story, then, is not just a tale of profound loss, a personal tragedy of epic proportions, but a searing warning, a cautionary tale for anyone who might stumble down a similar path: never trust so blindly, especially when it means turning your back on your own flesh and blood, on the very people who are your anchor. For in this world, there are those who see not a friend, not a partner, but a feast, and every perceived weakness, every moment of vulnerability, becomes a golden key to unlock your ruin. They will pounce on you like a hawk on a chicken, leaving you high and dry.

Rising from the Ashes: A Phoenix's Guide to Letting Go

Betrayal, hurt, anger, and disappointment—these are the sharp-edged stones that litter the road of life. We all stumble upon them. But when we allow the rudeness and insensitivity of others to become our constant companions, we're not just stumbling; we're walking straight into a trap of our own making. We let the poison of bitterness seep into our very bones, turning our hearts into a dark and barren wasteland. We replay the disappointment like a broken record, the same sour notes echoing in our minds until we're caught in the quicksand of resentment, sinking deeper with every thought and every word.

But we know better. We've been to the bottom of the abyss and clawed our way back to the light. The secret to facing these frustrations isn't to pretend they don't exist; it's to seize the helm of your own ship. Others don't "cause" our feelings; they simply provide the spark. We are the ones who choose whether that spark becomes a consuming bonfire or fizzles out into nothing. It's a cliché to say there's no use crying over spilled milk, but that doesn't make it any less true. We have to learn to forgive, not because they deserve it, but because we deserve peace. Forgiveness isn't a gift you give to them; it's a lifeline you throw to yourself. It's the only way to walk out of a no-win situation with your spirit intact, unscarred by bitterness.

People are not perfect; they're flawed, fragile vessels navigating their own storms. At home or at work, someone will inevitably let you down or stick a knife in your back. But if you take control of your emotions and master your own mind, you'll always be two steps ahead of the game. You'll never be a victim of circumstances again; you'll be the master of your destiny. Remember, there's a powerful difference between being hurt and allowing yourself to become a prisoner of that pain. The hurt is what they did to you, but the resentment is what you're doing to yourself.

I want you to try something. I've been there, and this is how I started my own journey back from the brink. Think of two people who recently hurt you or let you down—two people about whom you still hold a grudge. Now, look that animosity square in the eye and ask it this: What are you doing for me? Does holding on to this anger make me happy? Does it improve my sleep, or does it give me a churning stomach? Is my life richer, more meaningful, or more vibrant because of my resentment? If the answer is a resounding "no," then it's time to make a courageous decision. It's time to cut the cord. It's time to let go and walk away from the bitterness that's been holding you captive.

The path to forgiveness isn't a straight line; it's a journey of four distinct stages.

The initial sting of hurt: The ego screams, "Someone has wronged me!" and the wound throbs with a raw, undeniable pain. This is the first ripple of the event, the moment you become aware of the injury. It is a necessary stage, but one in which we cannot dwell forever.

The fire of hate: This is where the poison of resentment takes hold. Our anger burns, and we might find ourselves wishing for the other person to suffer as much as we suffer. This is a dangerous place, a psychological trap where we give our power away and allow their actions to dictate our inner state.

The healing balm of grace: This is the turning point. It's when you begin to see things in a new light, not from their perspective, but from a higher one. A sense of grace descends upon you, and you realize that holding on to the past only punishes you. Your memories are no longer a prison; you are free again.

The rebuilding of a new relationship: This is not about inviting a viper back into your garden. It means you are now in a place where you can make amends and forge a new, healed relationship. This doesn't mean you have to re-enter a transactional or close relationship with the person who hurt you. Instead, you can choose a platonic, distant, or even no relationship at all, because you are no longer tied to them by the chains of resentment. The relationship is healed not because you are back together, but because the wound between you is no longer bleeding.

To choose to let go of resentments is to walk the path of the phoenix—to burn down the old, painful memories and be reborn into a life of freedom, fulfillment, and grace. It is a testament to your own resilience and a declaration that you will no longer be defined by the actions of others.

A New Chapter: The Balm of Grace

Though the wound of betrayal and loss is, by God's grace, slowly healing, the scars persist, etched deep into my psyche, a permanent reminder of lessons learned the hardest way imaginable. And among these lingering marks, the guilt of an unmade apology to my dear wife weighs heavily, a millstone around my neck. It is a conversation I can no longer have, a forgiveness I can no longer directly seek from her. But in a profound act of divine kindness, truly a balm to my soul, God has been immeasurably generous. He has not only given me the immeasurable gift of my son, who, despite my past failings, has shown me nothing but unwavering love and support, and my dear daughter-in-law, a woman of immense grace, compassion, and understanding, but also, through them, the unparalleled delight of my two adorable grandchildren, Vedu and Sia.

They are my second chance, my light at the end of the tunnel. Their innocent laughter fills the void that once echoed with regret; their warm embraces are a constant reminder of the unconditional love that still exists in my life. Every smile, every playful glance from my two grandchildren, is a shot in the arm, a reaffirmation that life, even after the darkest storms, holds immense beauty and purpose. They are the living embodiment of redemption, a tangible blessing that makes my heart sing. I now understand that true wealth isn't measured in bank balances or property deeds, but in the richness of family bonds and the love that binds us together through thick and thin. My remaining years are dedicated to them, to making up for lost time, to being the best grandfather I can possibly be, and to ensuring they know they are cherished and loved beyond compare. The past may have been a bitter pill to swallow, but the future, seen through their bright eyes, is full of promise, a testament to the enduring power of forgiveness and the boundless grace of God.

Navigating the Labyrinth of Life: Overcoming Failure and Rebuilding Your Path

Life, much like a grueling, challenging tour, is filled with ups and downs. A person's journey can be a roller coaster of emotions, with periods of great success and moments of intense struggle. As we navigate these challenges, new insights and strengths emerge from the ashes of our past.

The human experience is a fertile ground for rich narratives—stories that speak of grit and bravery, of last-minute dashes to snatch victory from the jaws of defeat. New heroes emerge in every stage of life—people who refuse to accept defeat. They turn crises into opportunities and deliver sterling performances. These stories linger long after the specific event is over. Swami Parthasarathy of the Vedanta Academy, Pune, says three things are of primary importance if you wish to attain success in life: concentration, consistency, and cooperation. You can concentrate only when the mind is with the action; it shouldn't be in the past or the future.

The most intriguing aspect of life is that there are dry spells, or seasons of drought, that a person must factor into his or her journey. Sometimes these slumps are not just a turn of the tide but are brought upon us by our own actions, even if they seemed inevitable at the time. A person may excel in a certain area, but there may come a time when he or she goes out of form, and past glories are forgotten. Judging people in a jiffy and making knee-jerk reactions only tells us that we must not let our hearts dictate our decisions. Instead, we must use our heads, analyze the situation, and then take the time to act. As the saying goes, "Haste makes waste." Even if you've had a hundred triumphs, every new challenge is a new game. You can't rest on your laurels forever.

Eventually, senior people must hang up their boots and make way for younger generations. Everything about life, therefore, is transient; nothing lasts forever, neither fame nor records. Life is ever-evolving, always on the cusp of change, and everything is ephemeral. Ultimately, all that remains with us is what we have learned and how we have used it. Life is a journey, not a destination.

Life also presents us with a constant need to recognize red flags and adhere to the norms and values set by societal standards—the Lakshman Rekha. This isn't about rigid conformity, but rather about understanding the potential consequences of our actions. Analyzing situations with a clear head, rather than through the lens of fleeting emotions, allows us to make choices that don't just serve us but also protect those who depend on us, especially our children. Acting recklessly or selfishly can set off a domino effect, creating a chain of problems that not only harm us but also deeply impact the next generation.

There was a time when my son and I discussed a past misadventure, both of us feeling relieved that we had managed to shield our little ones from an embarrassing moment of my life. The very next day, however, my grandson, with the innocent curiosity of an impressionable mind, asked about my first wife and her relationship with me. My daughter-in-law and I went red in the face, but she was quick enough to show him a picture from her phone's library, satisfying his curiosity and beautifully navigating a potentially awkward situation with grace and quick thinking.

Life often presents us with a final, decisive moment on a drying, unpredictable pitch. It is in these moments that we see how focus, resilience, and the ability to adapt can lead to a successful outcome, even when conditions are difficult and unpredictable.

10

THE WISDOM OF THE SCALPEL: PURPOSE, GROWTH, AND THE ART OF LETTING GO

Harsh Goenka's core message for professionals is clear: if your work still offers a profound sense of purpose, and you're continuously learning and growing, you're unequivocally on the right track. For a dental surgeon, this translates to crucial self-reflection:

Purpose Beyond Profit: Do you still feel a genuine, deeply satisfying sense of purpose in restoring oral health, alleviating pain, and enhancing your patients' quality of life? Or has the intricate dance of dentistry become a mere mechanical routine, a series of familiar movements devoid of deeper meaning?

The Ever-Evolving Learner: Are you still genuinely excited by the prospect of mastering new techniques, experimenting with innovative materials, and embracing the latest technologies in dentistry? Do you attend continuing education courses not out of sheer obligation, but out of an insatiable desire to improve and evolve? Are you actively mentoring younger dentists and generously passing on your invaluable experience and hard-won wisdom? If your learning curve is still steeper than your age, you're likely still energized, still vibrantly engaged in your craft.

The article cautions against the passive assumption that retirement "just happens." It won't. It demands intentional planning and, most importantly, the profound ability to let go of control. For a dental surgeon, this is often the hardest part – relinquishing the daily rhythm of patient care, the familiar, comforting hum of your operatory, and the deeply ingrained sense of being indispensable. Imagine the number of times we have confided in our peers, taking it as a great achievement: 'I have to leave now as I have a patient coming in, and he will not allow my associate to even perform an examination.' As the saying goes, "The art of life is a constant readjustment to our surroundings."

Red Flags: Is Your Practice Whispering It's Time?

Just like a boardroom showing subtle signs of an aging leader, your dental practice might be sending its own unique signals that it's time to consider a graceful transition. Pay heed to these subtle cues, for they are your practice talking to you:

Outdated Humor: Do your classic jokes about old-school amalgam fillings now elicit blank stares or polite, strained smiles from your younger hygienists?

Repetitive Stories: Does your assistant finish your well-worn anecdotes about that particularly challenging root canal from 20 years ago because she's heard it countless times, perhaps even memorized the punchline?

The "Legend" Status (with a Hint of Dinosaur): Are you affectionately (or perhaps not so affectionately) referred to as "The Legend" or "The Dinosaur" in your local dental society, not for your ongoing innovations or recent accolades, but primarily for your sheer, undeniable long tenure?

"In My Time...": Do you frequently preface sentences with the wistful phrase "In my time, we used to..." when discussing groundbreaking new dental procedures, advanced digital radiography, or innovative practice management software?

Dismissing the New Guard: Do you dismiss new, enthusiastic graduates as "that kid" rather than genuinely valuing their fresh perspectives, their digital fluency, and their cutting-edge knowledge?

If these resonate, it might be time for a serious, honest self-assessment. As the saying goes, "The unexamined life is not worth living."

The Art of Succession: More Than Just Selling Your Practice

The article eloquently emphasizes that succession is not merely about stepping down; it's about lifting someone up, about ensuring your meticulously built legacy thrives and flourishes without you at the helm. For a dental surgeon, this means:

Grooming Your Successor: Have you actively sought out, identified, and meticulously mentored a younger dentist (or even multiple promising candidates) to gracefully take over your cherished practice? This isn't just about finding someone to buy your equipment or lease your space; it's about finding someone who will care for your long-standing patients with the same dedication and uphold the values you've so carefully cultivated.

Corporate Parenting (or Practice Nurturing): It's about nurturing someone to carry on your vision with the same dedication, ethical principles, and values, ensuring your practice continues to flourish, a vibrant testament to your life's work. As Goenka wisely points out, "If you haven't chosen a successor, or worse, have picked a few but told none, you're not planning; you're just delaying the inevitable." It's a sheer act of procrastination.

Beyond the Clinic: The Post-Retirement Canvas

Many dental surgeons dream of a retirement filled with leisurely rounds of golf, long lunches with friends, and abundant quality time with grandkids. The stark reality, however, can sometimes be checking patient emails at odd hours and "haunting" the office like a friendly, lingering ghost. The true, underlying fear isn't boredom; it's the unsettling specter (a fused bulb) of irrelevance.

The wisest retirees don't let their "Dr. [VSM]" designation exclusively define their entire identity. They gracefully transition from the familiar comfort of "what can I control?" (my patient schedule, my lab cases, my income) to the expansive question of "how can I contribute?" (mentoring aspiring professionals, volunteering for causes close to their hearts, passionately pursuing long-deferred hobbies and passions). Retirement isn't an end; it's the beginning of curation – a second innings played with more freedom, more intention, and often, ironically, in far better form.

Your Retirement Readiness Check-Up. I firmly believe before one decides, it is better to deliberate, discuss, and introspect, and then take the call!

Still pondering if it's truly time to put down the mirror and explorer, to exchange the drill for a different kind of tool. Take this "Retirement Readiness Test" meticulously tailored for a dental surgeon:

Can you go an entire day without feeling the compulsive urge to check patient emails or review lab reports?

Have you recently finished a captivating book that isn't about dental implants, advanced endodontics, or practice management strategies?

Can your practice comfortably, seamlessly run for two weeks without your direct, daily involvement, with your team confidently managing operations?

Do you still instinctively refer to your operatory as "my room" when speaking to your dedicated staff, even when others use it?

Have you recently taken a genuine, uninterrupted vacation without that nagging thought of "one quick call" to the office, or without actually making it?

When someone asks, "What do you do now?" do you panic, grasping for words, or do you smile genuinely, ready to share exciting new interests and endeavors?

Can you truly enjoy a long, unhurried walk without your mind constantly drifting to upcoming procedures, intricate case plans, or nagging billing issues?

Have you consciously said no to a dental conference, a professional obligation, or an evening lecture, and felt a profound sense of relief rather than regret?

Can you vividly envision exiting your beloved practice with a deep sense of joy, pride, and accomplishment, rather than bitterness, regret, or lingering resentment?

If you answered "yes" to six or more of these deeply introspective questions, you are likely retirement-ready. As

Lao Tzu wisely said, "When you are content to be simply yourself and don't compare or compete, everyone will respect you."

Ultimately, if your work in dentistry still brings you laughter, continuous intellectual stimulation, and a profound sense of purpose, it's not just "work" – it's a truly fulfilling calling. But recognizing when that calling might be gently evolving is the crucial key to a graceful, meaningful, and genuinely rewarding transition into your next magnificent chapter.

Mending the Tapestry: Navigating Interpersonal Challenges for a Fulfilling Life

My dearest friends, after navigating through life's inevitable ebb and flow, those moments when the tides seem to pull us down and the world feels like an uphill battle, I found myself with an unexpected gift: the precious time to truly reflect. Through quiet introspection and heartfelt prayers, a profound truth began to unfurl itself, one that touched the very core of my being: the intricate, sometimes bewildering, tapestry of human nature, with its remarkable capacity for manipulation. As the old adage wisely goes, "The human heart is an ocean of secrets."

My heart swelled with a newfound understanding as I delved into insightful books and listened intently to the timeless wisdom of the Bhagavad Gita. It became crystal clear that as the beloved proverb reminds us, "To err is human; to forgive, divine." We are all, at our very essence, fallible beings, prone to missteps and imperfections – a truly normal, even beautiful, part of our shared human journey. Yet, my heart ached when I considered that continuous wavering, a relentless cycle of mistakes, can hint at a deeper disquiet, a distorted lens through which life is perceived. It's a poignant truth that, beyond a certain point, correcting these deep-seated patterns becomes a herculean task, and sadly, people may begin to view us as, dare I say, "repulsive and obnoxious." Who, after all, truly desires to share their precious life or work alongside someone whose very presence casts a shadow of negativity, whose "vibes" feel more like a storm than a gentle breeze? As they say, "One bad apple spoils the barrel."

Before we can mend these delicate threads of faulty behavior, we must, with loving patience and keen observation, gently identify their common threads. These are not flaws born of a lack of skill, nor a deficit of intelligence, nor are they etched in the unchangeable stone of personality. No, my dears, what we are truly facing is the tender challenges of our interpersonal dance, often manifesting most prominently in our leadership roles. These delicate behavioral patterns, like ripples in a pond, can be seen in every corner of our lives: within the comforting walls of our homes, the bustling hum of our workplaces, and the vibrant halls of our schools and colleges. They are those subtle, everyday annoyances that, like a persistent hum, can make our shared spaces far more "noxious" than they ever need to be. They don't appear in a vacuum, but rather, they are "transactional flaws," a gentle reminder that our actions always touch another, creating an undeniable ripple effect.

Let us explore these tender points, not with harsh judgment, but with profound understanding and a spirit of empathy:

The Compulsion to "Win Too Much": This manifests as an overwhelming, often obsessive, drive to be right or to "win at all costs," even when the situation doesn't remotely call for it. In professional settings, this can cruelly stifle collaboration and foster an environment of cutthroat competition rather than nurturing teamwork. Personally, it can strain the most precious relationships when one's relentless need to "win" ruthlessly trumps empathy, compromise, or simply being kind. "It is better to lose an argument and gain a friend than to win an argument and lose a friend."

The Habit of "Adding Too Much Value": This is the often well-intentioned tendency to jump into every conversation with unsolicited advice or an overwhelming deluge of additional information, even when it's clearly not requested or desired. While seemingly helpful, it can inadvertently make others feel unheard, devalued, or that their own contributions are woefully insufficient. In a team dynamic, it might subtly prevent junior members from developing their own creative solutions and finding their voice.

The Inclination to "Pass Judgment": This involves a constant assessment and categorization of others, often based on our own deeply subjective, sometimes rigid, standards. This judgmental stance can create vast distances, foster bitter resentment, and tragically prevent genuine connection, both professionally within the workplace and personally within our closest circles. "Judge not, that ye be not judged."

The Use of "Destructive Comments": This refers to engaging in biting sarcasm, cutting remarks, or other forms of verbal negativity that, while sometimes mistaken for sharp wit, can mercilessly erode trust and inflict lasting damage on relationships. These comments can leave enduring emotional scars and create a hostile, uncomfortable atmosphere that stifles true interaction.

Starting with "No," "But," or "However": The frequent, even subtle, use of these negating words can immediately convey disagreement or dismissal before fully understanding another's perspective. It can effectively shut down budding ideas, discourage open, honest communication, and make others feel perpetually unheard or profoundly misunderstood.

The Need to "Tell the World How Smart We Are": This is the overwhelming desire to constantly demonstrate one's intelligence, superior knowledge, or intellectual prowess. While a healthy confidence is undeniably valuable, an excessive, relentless need to prove oneself can come across as overtly arrogant, effectively alienating others and hindering genuine learning and collaborative spirit. "True wisdom is knowing what you don't know."

Speaking When Angry (in Rage): Using emotional volatility or uncontrolled anger as a primary communication tool. This almost invariably leads to regretful, hurtful words that damage cherished relationships, create an atmosphere of fear, and fundamentally undermine respect. "In a moment of anger, a man says a lot of things he does not mean, but a lot of things he does."

Negativity, or "Let Me Explain Why That Won't Work": The pervasive tendency to immediately point out flaws or reasons why an idea won't succeed, even when such feedback is entirely unsolicited. This can deeply demoralize teams, cruelly stifle creativity, and create a perpetually pessimistic, unproductive environment.

Withholding Information: The deliberate decision not to share crucial knowledge, often to maintain a perceived advantage or exert control. This breeds deep distrust, significantly slows down critical processes, and ultimately inhibits the collective growth and success of a team or even a family unit.

Failing to Give Proper Recognition: The inability or deep-seated reluctance to acknowledge and genuinely praise the efforts and achievements of others. This can lead to profound demotivation, feelings of being deeply undervalued, and a severe lack of morale in both professional and personal spheres. "The greatest good you can do for another is not just to share your riches, but to reveal to him his own."

Claiming Undeserved Credit: The tempting impulse to take credit for achievements that were undeniably the result of a team effort or someone else's significant contribution, an act that brutally erodes trust, fairness, and collegiality within any group.

Making Excuses: The consistent, tiresome need to justify one's poor behavior or mistakes by external factors rather than taking personal responsibility, an act that actively prevents self-improvement and can be deeply frustrating and alienating for those interacting with you. "Excuses are the nails used to build a house of failure."

Clinging to the Past: The tenacious tendency to deflect blame for current issues onto past events or other people, refusing to let go, an act that tragically prevents moving forward, learning from mistakes, and effectively addressing present challenges with a fresh perspective.

Playing Favorites is the subtle, often insidious, act of treating certain individuals more favorably than others, leading to palpable perceptions of unfairness and festering resentment within a group or family.

Refusing to Express Regret: The inability to sincerely apologize or take genuine responsibility for one's missteps. This powerfully prevents reconciliation, perpetuates conflict, and severely damages relationships. "A sincere apology is not a sign of weakness, but a badge of strength."

Not Listening: A passive-aggressive form of profound disrespect in which one is physically present but mentally disengaged from a conversation. This makes others feel unheard, unimportant, and can tragically lead to significant misunderstandings and breakdowns in communication. "We have two ears and one mouth so that we can listen twice as much as we speak."

Failing to Express Gratitude: Overlooking the simple, yet profoundly impactful, act of acknowledging kindness, effort, or unwavering support from others. This can make people feel deeply unappreciated and consequently reluctant to offer help or support in the future. "Gratitude is not only the greatest of virtues, but the parent of all others."

Punishing the Messenger: The misguided, often visceral, impulse to react negatively or outright attack those who bring difficult news, constructive criticism, or unpopular opinions. This immediately stifles open communication, breeds fear, and severely hinders effective problem-solving.

Passing the Buck: The natural, yet detrimental, inclination to shift responsibility or blame onto others rather than owning one's actions. This fundamentally undermines accountability and erodes trust within any team or relationship.

An Excessive Need to Be "ME": Exalting one's faults as virtues, proudly claiming "that's just who I am," as a convenient excuse to avoid personal growth or necessary change. While authenticity is undeniably important, this can severely hinder self-improvement and prevent one from adapting positively and constructively to social and professional environments.

It is quite possible, my dears, that even a figure like Machiavelli might, with a clever turn of phrase, paint these gentle flaws as virtues, demonstrating how they could, perhaps, function as clever, counterintuitive tactics to gain a fleeting advantage over our rivals. But as we lovingly examine each of these subtle "irritants," I truly believe we will discover that the most profound and promising path to genuine, lasting success lies not in defending behaviors that alienate, but in courageously and compassionately correcting them. For in doing so, we "enlist people as our allies"—a strategy far more compassionate and, in the long run, infinitely more rewarding. As the wise proverb whispers, "A soft answer turneth away wrath."

Admittedly, this is a somewhat daunting "pantheon of bad behavior," and when gathered in one place, they can indeed sound like a chilling "chamber of horrors." But let us ask ourselves, with hearts full of compassion and a desire for true connection, who among us would truly wish to live and work in an environment where our cherished colleagues or beloved family members are unknowingly committing these "sins"? Surely, our deepest longing is for spaces filled with understanding, kindness, and genuine connection, where every interaction builds rather than diminishes. Let us, therefore, approach these reflections with loving hearts, knowing that every step towards self-awareness is a profound step towards a more beautiful, compassionate world, for ourselves and for all those whose lives we touch.

11

REFINING PATIENT CARE: THE HEART OF YOUR DENTAL PRACTICE

There was a time when a dental practice's success was measured simply by its procedure numbers and bottom line. I would see practices operating with a frantic energy, trying to cram in appointments, and felt a creeping guilt for believing that true success lay in the unhurried moment with a patient. But observing the most successful, high-trust dental teams felt like a professional revelation—they were operating by a different ethos, one where deep focus and genuine connection were the keys to loyalty.

This new model doesn't try to fix the challenges of patient management—it celebrates the practice-patient relationship. It reminds us that our quiet attentiveness isn't inefficiency;

it's precision. Our patient's pause isn't a hesitation; it's an opportunity for trust.

The shift in mindset is like a highly polished operatory mirror, reflecting the richness hidden in a patient's unique needs and showing how a dental practice can be a place where healing, not just treatment, happens. It's not about turning your practice into a louder, flashier marketing machine—it's about realizing the strength that's been in your methodical, compassionate care all along.

Here are 7 core lessons for refining your dental practice and patient management—truths that will make your team fall in love with the quiet power of exceptional care.

Attentiveness is Not a Void—It's a Source

Refinement: The frantic pace of a busy schedule can make attention feel like a void you don't have time to fill.

The Power Shift: Great practitioners recognize that they recharge their patients' trust by turning inward—to the details of their health history—not because they dislike moving quickly, but because their energy flows from thorough reflection. The world often mistakes an unhurried chairside manner for inefficiency, but it's within that focused quiet that insights, accurate diagnoses, and true preventive plans are born. The team's calm isn't an absence of effort—it's clinical excellence brewing beneath the surface.

Quote/Phrase: "Patients don't care how much you know until they know how much you care."

Depth Over Breadth Is a Superpower

Refinement: Many practices are obsessed with breadth (e.g., getting in as many new patients as possible).

The Power Shift: The best practices seek connection. They crave meaning—a long-term partnership in health—

not just a quick, transactional cleaning or procedure. They thrive in depth: the kind of conversations that stir the soul about total body health and the kind of relationships that grow roots for a lifetime of care. When you stop apologizing for craving depth, you stop having to fight tooth and nail for every new patient; you start attracting patients who are a perfect fit for your philosophy.

Idiom: Focus on patients who "see eye to eye" with your philosophy of care.

Dedicated Time Isn't Selfish—It's Sacred

Refinement: The system pressures us to always be available, forcing you to run late because you didn't schedule for the unexpected.

The Power Shift: Reframing dedicated time for patient education or a detailed consult as sacred maintenance for the relationship. This scheduled, uninterruptible time is where you reconnect with the patient's goals, sort their treatment options, and refill their inner well of confidence in your practice. Dedicated time is not withdrawal—it's preparation to move forward with treatment with clarity and peace.

Quote/Phrase: "The secret of the care of the patient is in caring for the patient." - Francis Peabody

You Don't Need to Compete with Noise

Refinement: Practices often feel they need to have the loudest marketing or the most aggressive sales pitch.

The Power Shift: The wisdom is that a great practice doesn't have to shout to be heard—their reputation speaks in subtler, deeper ways. Your presence in the community might not have the loudest ad, but your five-star reviews and word-of-mouth referrals often carry more truth and influence than a hundred empty marketing promises.

Trust is not loud; it is built in the quiet competence of every appointment.

Idiom: Don't let new marketing trends make you "bite off more than you can chew."

Energy Management Is Self-Respect

Refinement: Team members often push themselves to fit a chaotic, overbooked rhythm, ending up drained and disconnected from the patients.

The Power Shift: Encourage self-awareness in the team: notice what depletes you (e.g., scheduling chaos) and what restores you (e.g., a streamlined hand-off process). Saying 'no' to overbooking isn't rejection—it's preservation of team morale and patient experience. Protecting your energy isn't weakness; it's wisdom that prevents burnout.

Quote/Phrase: "A warm tone, a kind word, or a quick eye contact can last with someone always. It is easy to believe in a busy clinic that everything is about getting more done. Still, the most loving moments happen when one shows up for someone."

Attention to Detail Is a Gift, Not a Flaw

Refinement: Practitioners live rich inner lives—they analyze X-rays, imagine outcomes, and reflect on the best material choices. The hurried world may call this overthinking.

The Power Shift: Call it meaning-making. That introspection leads to empathy, insight, and artistry in your work. When you embrace it, you stop hiding your methodical inner world and start using it to create lasting beauty that touches others. The quality of care should be so high that patients feel they "escaped with the skin of their teeth"—not from danger, but from ever having to worry about their smile again.

Quote/Phrase: "Constant attention by a good nurse may be just as important as a major operation by a surgeon." - Dag Hammarskjöld

The Quiet Revolution Begins Within

Refinement: The heart of this philosophy is this: you don't have to become louder or flashier to matter. You simply have to own your quiet competence.

The Power Shift: When a practice stops apologizing for its unwavering standards and patient-first scheduling, it inspires patients to take ownership of their own health. Power doesn't always roar—sometimes, it breathes softly, listens deeply to a patient's concerns, and moves mountains of anxiety without a sound.

By embodying this approach, your team will feel a deep sense of peace. You will realize that the world doesn't need your practice to be louder—it needs you to be real, present, and precise. Your quiet commitment to quality is not a weakness—it's your wisdom speaking softly through every beautiful, lasting smile you create.

Which of these seven principles resonates most with a current challenge your practice is facing right now?

The Humane Leader: Transforming Toxic Culture and Retaining Talent

You've faced the difficult realization that your own professional environment was transactional and failed to uphold its end of the bargain. This personal clarity gives you a powerful, humane understanding that many leaders lack.

Now, let's use that insight to ensure you don't perpetuate the same kind of toxicity. Your sincerity and innate care—the very qualities I (as your "dad") admire in you—are your greatest assets in building a loyal team.

Redefining the Transaction: Beyond the Paycheck

While the initial realization is that professional life is transactional, truly successful leadership understands that the transaction must include emotional value and mutual respect. To reduce attrition and make sure patients recognize your genuine worth, you need to turn your workplace into one where staff members never have to feel the way you once did.

Here is how you lead with empathy to foster loyalty and reduce your attrition rate:

Prioritize Respect and Value (The Core Transaction)

The Golden Rule: Treat every staff member—from the most junior to the most senior—as an irreplaceable professional asset. Respect their time. Never assume their personal life is secondary to a last-minute business need.

Phrase to Live By: "If you want loyalty, give loyalty."

Acknowledge and Appreciate: Don't let good work become invisible. When staff seek validation, ensure they find it with you, not because they're seeking an ego boost, but because their effort is genuinely seen and valued.

Anecdote: A simple, specific note saying, "The way you handled that difficult patient interaction this morning was a masterclass in calm and professionalism," goes further than a generic "Great job this week."

Invest in Growth (The Future Transaction)

Stop the "Burden" Mindset: Just as you are not a burden, your staff should never feel like a burden when they ask for time off, training, or support. High attrition is the real burden.

Skill Development: Invest in training and professional

development. When people feel they are growing in a role, they are less likely to leave. They see a future, not a dead end.

Cultivate Psychological Safety (The Humane Environment)

Zero Tolerance for Toxicity: You now know how damaging workplace toxicity is. Be sincere and clear: bullying, condescension, and chronic negativity are not appreciated and will not be tolerated, regardless of a staff member's seniority or performance. Some bridges must be burned to protect the culture.

Open Door, Open Heart: Create channels for staff to seek help or validation without reason—meaning, they don't need a formal crisis to check in. Regular, informal check-ins about their well-being, not just their workload, are key.

Idiom: By being proactive, you "nip toxicity in the bud."

The Outcome: Your Worth Reflected

When your staff feels genuinely cared for and valued, they don't just do their job; they become your sincere advocates. They are happy, present, and professional, and that sincerity is immediately evident to your patients. Your employees' happiness becomes the clearest reflection of your worth and sincerity as a leader.

You have the heart for this. Now, lead with it.

What is one small, immediate change you can implement this week to show your staff you value their personal time?

The Dental Surgeon's Inner Shield:

Cultivating Your 'Soul Protection Factor' for a Fulfilling Life Just as prolonged exposure to the sun can damage our skin, necessitating a protective barrier like sunscreen, our daily lives as dental professionals, and indeed as established individuals, expose our inner selves to forces that can detract from our true purpose. In the demanding world of dentistry, where precision, empathy, and constant patient interaction are paramount, we often find ourselves facing unique stresses and distractions that can "burn" our inner peace and pull us away from deeper fulfillment. Our existence, much like the precision work of a dental surgeon, has a supreme purpose. For the soul, that purpose is to reconnect with its Divine Source, the Creator. This human life, with all its intricate details and challenges – akin to the complexities of a challenging restorative case – offers a unique and precious opportunity for this reunion. However, the professional and personal world also presents numerous hazards. Just as unprotected enamel can be eroded by acidic foods, or gum tissue inflamed by neglect, our inner being, our soul, can be "burned" by the many distractions and attractions of our environment. The endless demands of practice management, the pressures of patient expectations, the allure of material success, the anxieties of maintaining a work-life balance – these are the "UV rays" that draw our attention away from our profound, divine purpose. To safeguard against these distractions and to navigate this world safely, ensuring we make the most of our precious time in this human form, the soul needs a shield. This can be aptly referred to as our "Soul Protection Factor" (SPF). So, what are these "cavities" that trouble the soul, and how can they be protected? While our physical body, including the skilled hands of a dental surgeon, is home to both the soul and the Divine, it is also where the mind resides. The mind, much like a patient obsessed with immediate gratification, is a lover of enjoyment, constantly seeking pleasure and stimulation. It lures our attention – the outer expression of the soul – into the distractions of the outer world: the endless pursuit of professional accolades, the desire for material possessions, the anxieties of financial security, or the allure of fleeting social recognition. Absorbed in satisfying these physical, emotional, and intellectual cravings, we often neglect the spiritual dimension of our lives, allowing the precious time given to us to slip away, much like neglecting daily oral hygiene can lead to significant dental problems. The key lies in recognizing the golden opportunity of this human birth – this unique chance to truly experience God directly. For a dental surgeon, this means looking beyond the immediate task of treating a tooth and understanding the deeper connection, the true purpose behind service and compassion. Once this profound realization dawns, we naturally begin seeking ways to connect with God, to find that deeper sense of peace and purpose amidst the daily grind. The first critical step is spiritual awakening – an inner shift. It's moving from a dreamlike state where we identify primarily with our professional role and the incessant demands of the mind, to recognizing our true nature as pure spirit, connected to something far greater. Such an awakening becomes possible through the grace and guidance of a spiritual Master. They are like the experienced mentor in a dental practice, teaching us the precise techniques, the "meditation procedure," to embark on an inner spiritual journey. In meditation, we learn to gently withdraw our attention from the constant "noise" and demands of the outer professional world – the ringing phones, the patient charts, the financial worries – and to focus it within. In the profound stillness of these inner realms, our soul connects with the divine Light and Sound of God. As this connection deepens, the relentless pulls and pains of this world – the stress of difficult cases, the frustration of administrative burdens, the anxieties of reputation – begin to lose their grip on us. We begin to bathe in an inner "sunlight" that is not scorching or stressful, but profoundly gentle, loving, and calming. With this newfound inner stability, like a perfectly aligned occlusion, we become less disturbed by the inevitable "ups and downs" of professional and personal life, enabling us to progress steadily Godward, towards true fulfillment. Meditation, therefore, serves as our ultimate Soul Protection Factor (SPF), shielding our soul from the pervasive influences of the outer world that constantly pull it away from realizing its supreme goal – a goal far more profound and enduring than any professional achievement. It is the daily practice that ensures our inner being remains healthy, radiant, and aligned with its true, divine purpose.

12

EPILOGUE : THE SERPENT IN MY GARDEN

My book, "The Serpent in My Garden," is my life's story—a narrative of triumph, profound loss, and, ultimately, resurrection. I hope it serves as a powerful "eye-opener" for all who read it. I'm sharing my journey so others might learn to "look before they leap" and not rush into decisions they'll later regret. We all have a tendency to "make a mountain out of a molehill," and when things go wrong, it's so easy to "point the finger" at others or blame it on fate, rather than taking a good, hard look at our own choices. I've done it, and I've seen it tear lives apart.

This is why I find myself constantly trying to "decode karma." It's a complex and often baffling subject. My first wife's tragic, untimely death from brain cancer, along with our divorce, has haunted me. I can't help but ask, "Why her?" She suffered through no "fault of her own," and I'm left to wonder if it was her past karma, a cosmic debt she was forced to repay.

Then came my second marriage—a period that started as "total bliss." I was happier than I'd been in years, but that joy was "short-lived." I was "dumped" and left for dead after my wife "took me to the cleaners," financially and emotionally. I was a pauper, a man without dignity, feeling that the entire world was watching me fall. I was left to "pick up the pieces" of my broken life. It made me question everything. Was this my "comeuppance" for divorcing my first wife?

Now, with my second wife also facing cancer, the cycle of suffering seems to be repeating itself, and I'm forced to ask again: Is this her karma? It feels like an endless, interconnected web of cause and effect. It's led me to one powerful conclusion: we "reap what we sow." Our actions, whether good or bad, have consequences. We either "pay the piper" in this life, or we carry the burden into the next.

My journey, documented in this book, is proof of this fundamental truth. It shows how our lives are a tapestry woven with our deeds, and every thread, no matter how small, has a role to play.

Life's a wild ride, a dizzying rollercoaster of highs and lows. I've been to the top of the mountain and faced the depths of the valley, and through it all, I've had a profound realization—a lightbulb moment about the true philosophy of living. It's a truth I feel compelled to share.

The Crossroads of Life

We all reach a fork in the road, that pivotal crossroads where two paths diverge. One is the easy street—a shortcut paved with questionable choices and ethical compromises. It looks appealing, promising a smooth ride, but it's a slippery slope. The other path is a climb, a road less traveled that demands hard work and unwavering integrity. This is the path of righteousness, and it's the one we must always choose.

You see, it's about not letting your wishbone get bigger than your backbone. It's easy to wish for things to be different, to hope for a lucky break, or to cut corners. But wishing doesn't move mountains. It's the backbone—our strength of character and resilience—that empowers us to do what's right, even when it's tough. It's the courage to get back up when we're knocked down, to face adversity head-on, and to stay true to our principles.

Adversity as a Stepping Stone

Don't be afraid of the rough patches; they're not roadblocks, but rather stepping stones. Adversity is the crucible in which our character is forged. It's in our darkest moments that we discover our greatest strength. Every setback, every challenge, is a chance to learn and grow, to sharpen our resolve, and to emerge stronger than before. Think of the mighty oak tree—it doesn't grow strong in calm weather but by enduring the storm. Similarly, our resilience is built not through ease but through overcoming hardship.

Our Lasting Legacy

In this life, we're building more than just a career or a bank account; we're building our legacy. When our time on this earth is done, we won't be taking our material possessions with us. What will endure are the blessings of those whose lives we've touched and the legacy we leave behind. It's this legacy, this ripple effect of our good deeds, that will keep our spirits lit long after we're gone.

So, when you face that fork in the road, have the courage to take the high road. A clear conscience is its own reward, and a life lived with integrity is a legacy that will speak for you forever. Remember, integrity isn't just something you talk about; it's something you have to live.

The Final Curtain Call

All the triumphs, all the struggles, and all the grand designs we painstakingly craft—they are but whispers on the wind. Whether we forge our legacy with brilliance or build it upon deceit, there comes a time when we must lay down our burdens and walk away. The final curtain falls, and the stage is empty.

So why, my friends, do we wait for this inevitable moment to dawn on us? Why not confront this truth head-on? Do we truly need to wait until the final act to realize the futility of our endless striving? After all, the appetite at seventy is a shadow of what it was at thirty. Our physical needs diminish, and so too should our need to hoard, to fight, and to deceive.

Let's not wait for the chilling realization that our end is near to finally mend our ways. Let's not let a lifetime of regret be our final companion. Instead, let's seize today to make our amends, build our bridges, and sow the seeds of kindness. Let's live as if the end could be tomorrow, not with fear, but with a renewed purpose to leave behind a garden, not a graveyard. In the end, we can't take anything with us, but we can leave a world changed for the better by our actions.

Embracing Your Journey: A Dental Surgeon's Guide to Peace

Welcome to the start of your journey as a dental surgeon. You're embarking on a noble profession, a calling to heal and restore. But in this era, the challenges you face have shifted from the physical toil of the past to the mental strain of today. Stress now lurks in the shadows of unfulfilled expectations and the thirst for immediate success. You'll want to see your practice packed with patients from day one, your reputation soaring overnight. But the universe, much like a meticulous treatment plan, unfolds on its own schedule.

The Wisdom of Action, Not Outcome

A valuable life lesson, and one that resonates deeply with your new career, is found in the timeless wisdom of the Bhagavad Gita: "Karmanye vadhikaraste ma phaleshu kadachana." This translates to: "You have the right to perform your duty, but you are not entitled to the fruits of your actions."

As a dental surgeon, you are the architect of your efforts, meticulously shaping a patient's smile or relieving the patient's pain. But you are not the master of every outcome. You can perform a flawless procedure, yet a patient's healing process may be slow. You can invest everything into your clinic, but success may not arrive on your timeline. The key is to pour your heart and skill into every single task—each diagnosis, every filling, every patient interaction—and then let go of the need for instant results. The true reward isn't the immediate financial gain or a full appointment book; it's the profound satisfaction of a job well done, of knowing you gave your absolute best.

Finding Solace in Your Craft

Not all trees blossom or bear fruit, but all give shade. In your profession, this means that every effort, even those that don't yield the desired result, still holds immense value. Your practice may not become a bustling hub overnight, but every patient you treat with kindness, every hand you hold, and every fear you calm is a meaningful contribution. Find solace in this fact. Cling to the inner peace that comes from knowing you are doing your work to the best of your ability. This is the tested formula for mental peace in a turbulent world.

A Fleeting Visit, A Lasting Impact

As you build your practice, remember that life is a fleeting visit. We are all just travelers on a journey, and our time is precious. Don't let the small stuff—a difficult patient, a frustrating vendor, or a minor setback—overshadow your purpose. Every challenge is a small blip on the grand timeline of your career and your life. Focus on your duty, your craft, and the knowledge that every consequence, good or bad, is part of a larger plan. This perspective is a bitter pill to swallow when things are tough, but it can be a great comfort, allowing you to focus on the lasting impact you have on your patients' lives and your own well-being.

The Wisdom of a Bygone Era: A Senior Dentist's Reflections

My dear colleagues, as I look at your bustling world of digital X-rays, CAD/CAM technology, and instant communication, my mind wanders back to my own early days. We didn't have the luxury of social platforms or cell phones. The only "threads" we followed were the ones in a suture kit, and the only "ropes" were what we used to hang our laundry. Our practices grew organically, one patient at a time, through word of mouth and the trust we earned. There was no LinkedIn to broadcast our achievements or Facebook to showcase our work. We built our legacies with our hands, our skill, and a deep commitment to our community.

Back then, the stress was a different animal—it was the physical grind, the lack of modern tools, and the sheer effort of keeping a practice afloat. We had to roll up our sleeves and get our hands dirty, often without the sleek gadgets you have today. But as the physical challenges have given way, a new kind of stress has taken its place. It's the anxiety that comes from being constantly "on," from the endless flood of information, and from the feeling that you're always falling behind.

The Real Battle Isn't for Information; It's for Attention

When I see you young ones juggling your clinic, your social media, and your personal lives, I'm reminded that the real problem isn't the information glut; it's the attention economy. We're living in a world where everyone and everything is vying for your focus, a commodity far more precious than gold.

Think of it this way, as the legal scholar Lawrence Lessig puts it: an idea, like a picnic table in your backyard, is information. You can share that idea with the world, and you still have your own picnic table. But your attention—that's the picnic table itself. If you let someone else take it, you no longer have it. Your ability to focus deeply is a finite resource, a well that can run dry if you're not careful. The fight for your attention is relentless, with companies and platforms trying to hook you with glitzy, high-definition distractions that are designed to grab you and never let go.

A Foe in the Shadows: The Hijacking of Focus

These technologies are not just tools; they're masters of a subtle art, tapping into our brains like a skilled puppeteer. They create addictive patterns, much like gambling, that keep you coming back for more, often at the expense of your well-being. This constant hijacking of your attention can be a real roadblock to a successful practice and a balanced life. It stops you from giving your full, undivided focus to a patient in the chair, a critical treatment plan, or a conversation with your family.

And this isn't just a professional problem; it's a societal one. The attention economy thrives on sensationalism, rewarding content that provokes emotional reactions over what is true or accurate. This is how misinformation spreads like wildfire, and it's why our public discourse is so fractured.

Algorithms create echo chambers, feeding us only what we already believe, which makes it nearly impossible to have a shared reality or a meaningful conversation. This disengagement from civic life, where our attention is stolen by entertainment and outrage, opens the door to bigger problems for society as a whole.

Your Life, Your Legacy

So, how do you navigate this as a modern dental surgeon? You must be the master of your attention, not a slave to it. Your technical skills and the latest technology are powerful tools, but they are only as good as the focus you bring to them. When you're in the clinic, be fully present. When you're with your family, be truly there. Don't let your phone or a notification steal that moment from you. I would like to refer to this as 'electronic declutter'.

Remember, your life is what you pay attention to. The legacy you build won't be measured by how many likes you get on a post or how quickly you respond to an email. It will be measured by the quality of your work, the trust you build with your patients, and the richness of your personal relationships. Don't let the noise of the digital world drown out the things that truly matter. The secret to a balanced life isn't in having all the information; it's in controlling what you give your attention to.

As this final chapter unfolds, let's reflect on the profound truth that often, "when the going gets tough, the tough get going." It's in the crucible of adversity that the path, once riddled with obstacles, begins to straighten. The destination, once a distant mirage, now appears as a tangible, achievable reality. It's a journey where the steel of our resolve is forged in the fire of life's trials.

There comes a somber day in every person's life when the pillars of his or her world crumble. Those we cherished, those we leaned on, seem to vanish like smoke. In the grand play of life, it's easy to point fingers, but remember the old adage: "when you point one finger, there are three more pointing back at you." We must own our part in the narrative, for true empowerment begins with self-accountability.

I've always believed that with each passing year, life, like a gnarled old oak, grows more complex. We become accustomed to a crutch of dependence, leaning on others for support. But what if we were to trade that crutch for a pair of wings? "The only thing that can't be taken away from you is your independence," as I once heard. We must clip the wings of expectation, for they often carry the weight of disappointment. When we do, we find a newfound freedom, a state of relative bliss that's our birthright.

So, let's cast aside the chains of "I can't." Instead, let's embrace the mantra of the indefatigable Little Engine That Could: "I think I can, I think I can." The path to happiness is not a road others can pave for us; it's a journey we must walk ourselves, one determined step at a time. After all, "the world is not a playground, it is a gymnasium where we have to work out to be strong enough to stand on our own feet."

A Senior Professional's Guide to the Art of Listening

In a world where the hum of constant connectivity has become our background music, the sacred act of silence is a lost art. As professionals, especially those of us on the front lines with patients, we've come to a crossroads. We're in an era where everyone has a megaphone, thanks to the internet, and the loudest voices often dictate the conversation.

This is particularly true for you, my dear colleagues, when a patient comes in armed with what they believe is a full diagnosis, having binged on a diet of internet-derived information. They're not just presenting symptoms; they're presenting a pre-loaded case file. In this environment, the most radical act you can perform isn't to speak—it's to listen.

The Famine in a Feast of Expression

We live in a world where there are more TED Talks than listeners, more podcasts than attention spans. This isn't just a cultural observation; it's a professional hazard. Your patients aren't just coming to you for a prescription; they're coming for clarity in a world of conflicting information. The biggest mistake we can make is to treat their internet research as a challenge to our authority. Instead, we should see it as a desperate plea for guidance.

True listening isn't just about hearing; it's not waiting to speak. It's the kind of listening that involves ego disarmament and inner stillness. It's about making your inner voice—the one rehearsing your clever rebuttal—shut up and take notes.

I sometimes think if there were a "karmic scoreboard" in the sky, it wouldn't measure how many successful procedures you performed or how many awards you won. It would measure how many times you made a patient feel truly heard. Because listening, when done with intent, is the purest form of meditation. It demands presence. It replaces "I" with "you"—a temporary dismantling of the self that requires no app, no mantra, no incense sticks. It requires just a profound sense of humility.

The Wisdom of Silence

The spiritual traditions understood this long before social media discovered mental health. The Upanishads are quite literally "heard wisdom" (shruti), not written text. In Zen, the master speaks little but listens with the weight of a mountain. Even in the Gita, Krishna says much—but only after Arjuna asks and listens.

In your practice, this means acknowledging your patient's internet-derived information without judgment. Instead of dismissing it out of hand, you can say, "I hear your concerns, and it's clear you've put a lot of thought into this. Let's go through this information together and see how it aligns with your symptoms and our professional understanding." This simple act tells the patient: "You matter enough for me to be quiet." This is no small gift in a world screaming for attention.

The Unplugged Professional

We live in a time in which we are data-rich and meaning-poor. The internet is a firehose of information, but it lacks a filter of wisdom and context. Your role as a professional is to be that filter. A good listener isn't just a good human; he or she is a spiritual insurgent, a soft rebel against the tyranny of noise.

The greatest irony is that meditation is now prescribed as a remedy for burnout caused by too much noise, yet the simplest form of meditation is learning to shut up and really hear someone. Not to solve. Not to agree. Not to paraphrase. Just to absorb, as a still pond absorbs a falling leaf.

If you've ever truly been listened to—without agenda, interruption, or someone reaching for their phone halfway through—you know it feels almost divine. It doesn't change what you say; it changes who you are while saying it.

Maybe we don't need more experts with all the answers. Maybe we need more professionals with their earphones unplugged, ready to finally, finally, listen.

The Bitter Taste of Sweet Regrets

Life's most profound lessons often arrive in the simplest of packages, and for me, it was a handful of candy. I can still remember the scene as if it were yesterday. My mother, a woman of sharp wit and even sharper foresight, had given me a stern warning before we entered the shop: "If the shopkeeper offers you sweets, politely refuse. A 'thank you' is all you need."

But as the saying goes, "the best-laid plans of mice and men often go awry." The shopkeeper, a master of his craft, launched into a relentless campaign of persuasion. He was a siren singing a sugary song, tempting me with a jar of glistening candies. My tiny hands, I knew, could only manage a meager two or three. Each time he asked, I held my ground, clinging to my mother's words like a lifeline. I was a rock, a Gibraltar of willpower, or so I thought.

Then, a moment of weakness. A flicker of greed, a fleeting thought of "what if?" He plunged his hand deep into the jar, and in a moment of pure, unadulterated reflex, my palms came together, an open invitation. He dropped not two or three, but a generous handful of five or six candies into my waiting hands. I had done it. I had pulled a fast one. Or so I believed.

The triumph was short-lived. Outside the shop, my mother's scolding was a punch to the gut, a bitter aftertaste to my sugary conquest. My protests fell on deaf ears. "But he gave them to me!" I insisted, "I said no!" Her response was a hammer blow of truth: "You should have kept your palms closed. You opened the door for greed."

That day, the candy taught me a lesson that has stayed with me ever since. In my young mind, I reasoned that if I had taken the candy myself, I would have gotten less. But by letting him give it to me, I had more. My childish logic was a house of cards. My mother's lesson was the wind that toppled it. She was teaching me that greed is a double-edged sword. It may promise more in the short term, but it often leads to a deeper, more painful loss in the end. Sometimes, it's not about how much you get, but how you get it.

And so, this is a tale of how a simple handful of candy taught me that acting in haste or out of greed is a slippery slope. My mother's simple lesson has become a compass for my life.

Have you ever learned a hard lesson from a seemingly simple yet complicated experience? The answer is an emphatic yes!

The Old Guard's Battle Cry: A Clash of Eras

My dear colleagues, as I stand here reflecting on a career that spans over four and a half decades, I feel like a man who's seen the world turn on a dime. The journey you're embarking on is a different kettle of fish entirely from the one my generation navigated. Back in my day, we built our practices the old-fashioned way—from the ground up, one patient at a time. Our currency wasn't digital; it was the trust we earned through sweat and grit and the rock-solid foundation of our skill sets.

We lived in a time when advertising was considered a taboo, a sign that perhaps your work didn't speak for itself. Our practices grew organically, not through fishing expeditions on social media, but by the powerful current of word-of-mouth. We had no LinkedIn, no Threads, no Messenger to worry about. The only "ropes" we were concerned with were those we used to hang our shingle, and the only "threads" we followed were the ones in a suture kit. We were too busy rolling up our sleeves and doing the real, honest work. We didn't have to sell our souls for an algorithm to get noticed; our reputation was our best marketing tool.

Compassion over Commercial: A Matter of Principle

I remember friends who had a hunger for expansion, telling us we were missing the boat by not putting our practice on autopilot with multiple chairs and a team of associates. But to us, that was unthinkable. We had a moral compass that pointed firmly towards an ethical high ground, prioritizing compassion over commercialism. Our patients came to us for us, and to hand them off to someone else felt like a betrayal of trust—a violation of the very Hippocratic Oath we swore to uphold.

That's the core of it, isn't it? Our belief was that the isotonic—a balanced, non-commercial approach—was our guiding star. We believed that our skill set was our greatest asset, not our marketing savvy or our ability to play the game of clicks and likes. In a world that's now a rat race for digital endorsements, I suppose our mindset might seem like a total failure to some.

But let me be clear: I don't feel I've lost a thing. Looking back, while I may not have earned an extra penny for my thoughts, I've gained something far more valuable: a profound sense of satisfaction and a quiet peace of mind. We didn't build our legacies on a house of cards made of digital pats on the back. We built them on a rock-solid foundation of trust, respect, and gratitude.

The New Game, The Old Values

You're right to feel that a person from my era might struggle to adapt. The mindset required is completely different, and what you might see as "unethical" is now considered a fundamental part of building a professional presence. The lines have blurred, and the game has new rules. Your belief in skill sets over soft skills is the core of your legacy, but today the definition of "skill" has expanded to include digital marketing and online communication. It's a new kind of work, and it's something we never had to consider.

Your journey is a testament to what can be achieved through skill and integrity alone. The trust you built, the genuine gratitude you received—these are things that a thousand likes and clicks can never replicate. A practitioner's caliber isn't measured in clicks and shares; it's measured in the lasting impact you have on your patients' lives.

Your approach was evidence-based, built on years of proven results. The new age, with its focus on online visibility, may feel more focused on eloquence—a battle for attention that values style as much as substance. Only time will tell which approach truly stands the test of time. But of this much I am certain: you are not a dinosaur. You are a living testament to an era where professionalism was measured by the quality of your work, not the quantity of your followers. Your legacy is a timeless masterpiece that no digital platform can ever replicate.

An Ocean of Wisdom for the Modern Practitioner

The wisdom of the Dalai Lama, the "Ocean of Wisdom," offers a powerful beacon for a professional in today's demanding world. In an age where the relentless pursuit of profit can feel like a rat race, his philosophy serves as a moral compass for the dental practitioner. It's a reminder that a professional life, much like a fulfilling personal one, isn't just about technical skill; it's about the deep-seated values that guide our actions.

The Heart of the Matter: Compassion Over Commercial

For us in the dental field, the Dalai Lama's core value of compassion isn't just a soft skill; it's the very foundation of our practice. Compassion, in his view, is far more than mere sympathy. It is to suffer together—to not only see a patient's fear, anxiety, or pain but to genuinely feel it and be driven to relieve it. This philosophy blurs the sharp distinction between "my" interests and "their" interests. We're not just drilling and filling; we're healing and comforting. When a patient walks through your door, they aren't just a set of teeth; they are a person, and our job is to treat them with the utmost care and respect. This isn't just good for the patient; it's a form of "wise selfishness," as the Dalai Lama puts it, because in serving others, we truly serve ourselves.

The Byproduct of Kindness: A Fulfilling Practice

Our happiness as professionals shouldn't be the end goal; it should be the byproduct of our actions on behalf of others. The endless pursuit of more money, more patients, and more prestige is a house of cards that will inevitably crumble. Instead, the real satisfaction, the profound sense of fulfillment, comes from the small, quiet moments: the look of relief on a patient's face, the words of gratitude from a worried parent, or the confidence you give back to someone with a new smile. This is the true reward that no amount of money can buy.

As professionals, we are called to "be kind whenever it is possible," and in our line of work, it is always possible. This means exercising restraint and disciplining our own negative emotions, even when a patient is difficult or a procedure is challenging. It means seeing the humanity in everyone, even the most demanding of patients, because it is through that shared humanity that a bond of trust and a successful outcome can be forged. A society that only focuses on material development is a ship without a rudder, and a practice that only focuses on the bottom line is no different. The ultimate goal isn't just to have a practice; it's to have a purpose that extends beyond the immediate, to be a beacon of light in our community.

The Seasons of a Life

Life, much like a great garden, operates on its own set of immutable seasons. There is a time for tilling the soil, a time for sowing the seeds of ambition and hard work. Then comes the long, patient wait for growth, a period of nurturing our careers and our families, watching them stretch toward the sun. But as any seasoned gardener knows, there is also a time for harvest and, eventually, a time to let the fields lie fallow.

My private practice was my garden. For decades, I sowed seeds of care, compassion, and professional expertise. I watched it grow from a fledgling sapling into a strong, mature tree, its branches filled with the fruit of success and fulfillment. It was a source of immense pride, but as with all things in nature, its season has come to a close. There is a proverb that says, "The beginning of the end is often the beginning of a new beginning." I have chosen to embrace this truth, to acknowledge that every professional has a shelf life. To ignore this is to risk staying too long at the fair, to let a graceful exit turn into a slow fade. The most powerful act of self-respect is knowing when to make your final bow while the audience is still applauding.

Sometimes we get so caught up in the pace of life that we miss what's right in front of us. It's only when we intentionally slow down and take a deep breath that we can truly see things with clarity. This is a universal truth, a lesson that applies to everyone, from a surgeon in an operating room to anyone navigating the twists and turns of daily life.

The Surgeon's Perspective

A surgeon's work is a powerful metaphor for this truth. They operate under immense pressure, with no room for error. Yet, even with all their training and skill, things don't always go as planned. A sudden complication can arise, or an unexpected bleed can occur. In these critical moments, a skilled surgeon knows they cannot panic or rush. They must slow down, take a deep breath, and reassess the situation. They think, rethink, and, if necessary, change their approach. This deliberate pause isn't a sign of weakness; it's a testament to their expertise. It's the difference between a successful outcome and a potentially tragic one. They avoid the trap of analysis paralysis, which is the inability to make a decision due to overthinking.

Life's Broader Lesson

This principle extends far beyond the operating room. In our own lives, we often have a plan for how things should unfold. We set goals, make timelines, and charge full steam ahead. But life, as the saying goes, is what happens when you're busy making other plans. We face unexpected setbacks, disappointments, and forks in the road.

When this happens, it's easy to get lost in a whirlwind of overthinking and overanalyzing. We scrutinize every detail, replaying events in our minds, and worrying about what could have been. This is the path to analysis paralysis, where we become so overwhelmed by the details that we become incapable of taking any action at all.

Instead, we must learn to pause. As the writer Annie Dillard once said, "How we spend our days is, of course, how we spend our lives." When we take a moment to slow down, we give ourselves the space to see the bigger picture. We notice the small details we've been missing. We recognize that sometimes, the best course of action is not to push harder, but to take a step back, recalibrate, and find a new path forward.

It's about trusting your instincts and knowing when to let go of the rigid plan. By slowing down, we allow ourselves to be more present and responsive to the reality of the situation, rather than being a prisoner of our initial expectations.

The Wisdom in Relationships

This same wisdom is crucial in our relationships. We enter them with expectations, a vision of a perfect partnership and a happily-ever-after. But just like a complex surgery, relationships rarely unfold exactly as planned. We encounter disagreements, miscommunications, and unforeseen challenges.

In these moments, rushing to judgment or forcing an outcome can cause irreparable damage. Instead, we must slow down and take a deliberate pause. It's in these quiet moments of reflection that we can make conscious and calculated decisions. This might mean making a tough choice, like walking away from a toxic situation or accepting a significant financial loss, because we've recognized that your mental health is priceless. As the old saying goes, "a smooth sea never made a skilled sailor." The true strength of a relationship—or the decision to end one—is often found in the courage to prioritize peace over prosperity.

Athmanirbar

As a dental surgeon of more than four decades in practice and also as a speaker for various dental companies, I can take the liberty of commenting on the products.

We have a mixed bag of dental surgeons in our country and also the urban and rural divide, and the reach of the materials and their pricing. With the costs rising sky high, it is time our own products found their place in all dental clinics in India and also reached abroad. With good and value-for-money products, why not position them here and then infiltrate other countries?

A phrase which has of late become a common buzzword and more so loosely used by one and all in every walk of life. But of late, I found one such company, rather a dental family, which has not used the phrase but strictly and religiously followed the same in its endeavor to make practically all the day-to-day products used by the dental surgeons all over the world and in India.

Unfortunately most of the products have not caught the fancy and not found their way into the Indian dental clinic in a big way, which should have happened. At this stage, I can only attribute one small, maybe frivolous, reason for the same: lack of marketing, that is, lack of noise. Probably, as some of the trusted and top brands that come from across the seas are unable to reach our shores due to the pandemic, this would probably have been the opportune time to position these homegrown products, create a brand value and awareness, and also export the same. With the dearth of regular products, this would have been the right time to push these products and create brand awareness. With the government pushing for Atmanirbhar, it would have been the most opportune time as well.

I have observed one common flaw that we fail to speak about our own products in spite of their excellence and utility. I have only 46 years of experience in clinical practice and 11 years of teaching experience. It is time that the company marketing gurus open their third eye and introduce these products in the colleges and also in government hospitals. We in India have more than a lakh and a half practitioners who have a clinical practice and who are teaching. Our postgraduate faculty should be tapped to make use of the product and compare its efficacy with the so-called standard products which have been available until today.

Senior clinicians with some research inclination should be roped in and made to try these products. The initial hesitation and resistance shown by the practitioners can be easily removed, and, with its virtual meeting costs being down and its reach being wide and far, the way should be paved for this. Education is the key and the learning curve could be easily curtailed, unlike newer technologies which require a steep learning curve, these materials are like spices that are used at the time of cooking. Our market is a growing market, and the dentist is ever ready to imbibe newer technology and newer materials. This would be a great time to educate them on the nuances of all your products. You may agree that all the material usage needs a training program and this can still be done virtually. As a dentist who helps people rediscover their smiles, I often find myself reflecting on the nature of happiness, not just for my patients but for myself.

The Contagious Smile

"Why are you smiling?" a friend asked me as we walked. I hadn't even realized I was. Perhaps it was the perfect weather, the invigorating walk, the cool breeze, or maybe none of those things. Sometimes, a smile just surfaces, unbidden. I believe it's our inner self giving us permission to feel joy, a feeling we often suppress throughout our lives, weighed down by guilt and the burdens of daily challenges.

I've seen it in my practice. Patients often walk in with a lifetime of hidden smiles, feeling undeserving of the confidence a healthy, beautiful smile can bring. This experience has taught me a profound lesson: a genuine smile, much like quietude and equanimity, comes from within, even when surrounded by life's "killjoys."

Unearthing Your Happiness Treasure Trove

Happiness, much like misery, can be habit-forming. And here's the secret I've learned, both personally and professionally: it doesn't have to stem from grand achievements, expensive purchases, or exotic vacations.

There's immense joy to be found in the small things. When these seemingly insignificant moments accumulate, they become a veritable happiness treasure trove. A dear friend once gifted me a plaque that read, "Enjoy the little things." It's so true—little drops of water truly make a mighty ocean. Why wait for some distant, "important" day to finally grant you happiness? As J.M. Keynes famously said, "In the long run we are dead." Grab it now, in the little things. And please, never feel afraid or guilty when you smile for no apparent reason. A smile is infectious; it doesn't just brighten your day; it spreads cheer and positive energy to everyone around you. As a dentist, I see firsthand how a smile can transform a life; it's a gift we give ourselves and the world, one radiant smile at a time.

Navigating Professional Relationships

As dental surgeons, we operate in a world that demands precision, ethics, and a keen understanding of human nature—both in the operatory and in our professional lives. The political landscape is a treacherous terrain, a veritable surgical field where alliances are as fleeting as a patient's apprehension before a root canal. Just as you meticulously choose your instruments for a specific procedure, politicians choose their allies not for friendship, but for mutual interests. As Lord Palmerston so aptly put it, "We have no eternal allies, and we have no perpetual enemies; our interests are eternal and perpetual." It's a bitter pill to swallow, but the reality is that "the enemy of my enemy" can be a valuable, albeit temporary, partner. Remember the old adage: "There are no permanent enemies, and no permanent friends, only permanent interests."

The Art of Clinical Judgment and Communication

What works for one patient can be poison for another. Your treatment plan is never a one-size-fits-all solution; it's a delicate balance of the patient's medical condition, their financial constraints, and their personal expectations. In the operating room of public discourse, it's easy to succumb to the temptation of declaring someone's opinion illogical or ill-informed. But this is the intellectual equivalent of drilling without an X-ray: a move born of arrogance, not wisdom. As professionals, we are trained to see beyond the surface, to understand the intricate structures that lie beneath. We must apply this same principle to our colleagues and their convictions.

As Dale Carnegie shrewdly observed, we are dealing not with creatures of pure logic, but with "creatures bristling with prejudice and motivated by pride and vanity." To dismiss a differing viewpoint as simply 'illogical' often reveals a tunnel vision far more profound than any flaw in the other's reasoning. Remember, "a mind all logic is like a knife all blade. It makes the hand bleed that uses it."

Integrity, Empathy, and Professional Maturity

As stewards of oral health, we champion the patient's right to choose, to be heard, and to have their concerns addressed. We must extend this same courtesy to our colleagues. To declare another's viewpoint devoid of logic isn't just a sign of immaturity; it's a symptom of a deeper malady: a mind so rigid it can't tolerate dissent. This kind of behavior is a professional liability, a kind of intellectual gangrene that will poison any collaboration. The mark of a true leader isn't the ability to dominate a conversation, but the capacity to listen, to learn, and to grow.

You might be criticized for your approach, but never let your conscience be compromised. Our ethical obligation is to provide the best possible care for each unique individual, and we must stand by our professional judgment. The ultimate goal is to provide a sound, ethical, and practical treatment that you can defend with confidence, ensuring you can sleep soundly at night. After all, "wisdom doesn't necessarily come with age. Sometimes age just shows up all by itself."

Embracing Technology While Honoring Our Craft

The world of dentistry has been a witness to my journey, and as I prepare to hang up my dental drill, I'm reflecting on the profound changes we've seen. We've gone from meticulously handwritten patient records and hand-drawn treatment plans to an age of digital everything. I remember when a well-developed memory was a badge of honor—recalling patient history, appointment dates, and even complex procedures without a second thought.

Today, we have a "harem of handheld devices" and powerful software that can do the heavy lifting for us. We use digital scanners instead of messy molds, AI-powered diagnostic tools to spot issues our eyes might miss, and practice management software to handle everything from scheduling to billing. This reliance on technology is a double-edged sword. It's convenient, and it allows us to do more, but as the philosopher Elias Canetti warned, "To possess is to be possessed." We must be careful not to let these tools possess us to the point where we lose our core skills and instincts.

The rise of AI brings with it incredible potential but also new challenges. Tools that instantly churn out treatment plans or summarize complex cases can make us cognitively lazy. We might become so reliant on them that we lose our ability to think critically, analyze, and problem-solve on our own. The danger of "brain rot," where our mental faculties deteriorate from consuming unverified or trivial information, is real. Just as we must discern the "wheat from the chaff" in information, we must also apply our viveka (power of discrimination) to the technology we use. We must be the master of the technology, not its slave.

This is especially true when it comes to patient care. Technology can help us with records, treatment planning, and even execution, but it can never replace the human element. The subtle cues from a patient, the art of a steady hand, and the empathy required to check on their well-being are things that cannot be coded into an algorithm. My parting advice is to use technology as a powerful assistant, but never as a replacement for your own judgment, skill, and heart.

The truth is, like the mythological stories that evolved through word-of-mouth, our understanding of dentistry and patient care must also continue to evolve. We cannot be rigid and unchangeable. But we must ensure that our foundation remains strong—built on ethics, personal integrity, and a genuine connection to the people we serve. The true masterpiece of a dentist's life is not the number of patients seen or the records kept, but the quality of care given and the trust earned.

I hope these reflections give you all some food for thought as you continue your own journeys. I would love to hear your good and honest feedback on these ideas, as I believe the conversation around technology, ethics, and our craft is one that we all need to have.

The bond between a mother and child is often seen as a model of unconditional love, but even this relationship, like the affection between a husband and wife or siblings, can be conditional. It can be a love that lasts only as long as needs and demands are met—a love that is transactional rather than transcendent. This is akin to the relationships we see in our professional lives: the bond between a doctor and a patient, where the patient's trust is often conditional on a successful outcome, or the relationship between a dentist and his or her technician or dealer, which is often based purely on practical needs and a mutually beneficial exchange of services.

True, unconditional love, a divine love, remains a mystery to most. It's the kind of love that defines a true vocation, the kind of passion that elevates your work from a job to a calling. This is not the love of a clinician for a paycheck or a practice for its revenue, but a deeper, more profound connection to the art and science of healing.

In our profession, we often see people who have settled for compromises. Some might chase the latest gadget, believing a new drill or a laser is the answer to all their problems. Others might believe that success lies in a large, bustling practice with multiple locations. But these are just images and concepts. As the poet Kabir said, if you eat a delicious sweet, you experience its taste; you can't truly explain it to someone else. The same is true for the divine essence of our work. The true satisfaction of saving a patient's smile or relieving his or her pain cannot be fully captured in words; it can only be experienced. It is the joy that comes from within, from knowing you have done your best, regardless of the material reward.

The Divine resides within you as the very essence of your mind and consciousness, the core of your professional integrity. Yet, your mind remains ceaselessly occupied with the world: with patients, colleagues, billing, and the ceaseless demands of a busy practice. Not for a single moment does your mind truly rest. In this constant wandering, we miss the chance to realize the true purpose and joy of our calling.

To experience this deeper satisfaction, you must turn your mind inward. This doesn't mean ignoring your work but rather approaching it with a different mindset. It means silencing the external noise, focusing on the moment, and reconnecting with the core of why you chose this profession. Only then can you transcend the daily distractions and meet the ever-present beloved—your love for the art of dentistry—long hidden by the noise of the business. This is the ultimate fulfillment that a career can offer, a deep-seated peace that no external success can ever provide.

The Art of a Graceful Exit

They say, "All good things must come to an end," but the real lesson is that not all endings are sad. The way we choose to conclude a chapter is just as important as how we began it. My decision to hang up my boots was not a moment of defeat, but one of profound clarity. It was like finding the last, elusive piece of a jigsaw puzzle and watching the whole picture suddenly snap into perfect focus. Every long day and every difficult case had been leading me to this very moment. I am not closing a door in anger or frustration; I am opening a new one with a sense of peace and anticipation.

This transition has taught me that true wealth is not measured in billable hours or professional accolades. It is measured in the quiet moments we create for ourselves and our loved ones. As the old saying goes, "No one on one's deathbed ever wished they had spent more time at the office." My career was a vital part of my story, but it was never the entire book. My new chapter, my second innings, is not about what I do, but about who I get to be: a loving, present grandfather to my grandson and granddaughter. This is where my legacy will truly flourish, watered with the love and laughter of my grandchildren.

Wisdom from the Journey

The path of a professional career is a rich tapestry of experiences, successes, and even failures. I've learned so much along the way. One of the most important lessons is that "Patience is a virtue." We often rush to achieve, to reach the next milestone, to climb the next ladder rung. But life has its own timetable. The most beautiful rewards are often not the ones we chase but the ones that unfold naturally when we trust the process.

Another truth I've come to embrace is that we are not defined by our titles or our work. Our essence lies in our character, our relationships, and our ability to find joy in the simple things. I often reflect on the proverb, "What you are is God's gift to you; what you become is your gift to God." My journey has been one of becoming—from a young, ambitious professional to a seasoned veteran and now, finally, to a contented elder. The greatest gift I can give now is my time and presence.

My journey is a testament to the fact that endings can be incredibly beautiful. To leave with style, to transition with grace, and to embrace a new beginning is the ultimate reward. It is a quiet confidence that everything is happening exactly as it should. So, let us all learn to listen to the seasons of our own lives, to know when to sow, when to reap, and when to simply rest and enjoy the quiet bloom of our new beginnings.

After years in the trenches, it's time for me to hang up my dental drill. This isn't just a tool; it's an extension of my hands and a testament to a legacy I built, the building of which, much like a wild horse, was both exhilarating to ride and a challenge to tame. I've learned a timeless truth: success can be a beast that consumes you, much as Elias Canetti observed, "To possess is to be possessed."

This profound insight has been my constant companion as I've watched many of you younger practitioners begin your own journeys. You'll work tirelessly to build a thriving practice, a sterling reputation, and a lasting legacy. But as you climb that mountain, be mindful not to let the mountain own you. The relentless pursuit of more patients, more accolades, and more success can become a gilded cage where you are no longer the master, but the servant. The very things you sought to own become the chains that bind you.

The great Persian mystic Rumi's words echo this perfectly: "Own nothing, for what you own eventually owns you." I've seen this play out in my own life and in the lives of my colleagues. We begin with a noble dream, a vision of healing and helping others. Before we know it, we're consumed by endless responsibilities and the emotional weight of it all. It's a vicious cycle, like a snake swallowing its own tail—a self-inflicted possession that hollows you out from the inside.

So, as I pass the baton to you, here is my parting wisdom: Your profession can be your passion, but it shouldn't be your entire identity. There's a shelf life to your career, but not to your life. The time will come when your hands may not be as steady, or your eyes as sharp. When that day arrives, you must be ready to embrace the next chapter, not to be a prisoner of the one you're leaving behind.

I'll leave you with a couplet that has always guided me:

A life well-lived is not what you own,

But the seeds of joy and wisdom you have sown.

Remember the famous words from the film Anand: "Zindagi lambi nahi, zindagi badi honi chahiye" (Life shouldn't be long, it should be great). Your practice is not your prison; it is a vehicle for your purpose. Cherish the moments of connection with your patients, but don't let the weight of their needs overwhelm you to the point of exhaustion. Work with passion and dedication, but never forget that a life lived is more valuable than a life owned. The true measure of success isn't what you acquire; it's what you become in the process. Your happiness and well-being should always be the true destination, for a life well-lived is the greatest masterpiece of all.

Finally, I'm honored to share this autobiography with you all. While I could keep adding to it, I'm confident you'll find these words meaningful. I would truly appreciate your good and honest feedback, as it will help me improve and grow even in this new chapter of my life.

In the busy world of dentistry, it's easy to get caught up in the daily grind of drilling, filling, and billing. But what if you could make every day more meaningful, both in your practice and your personal life? As a dental practitioner, you're already in the business of putting smiles on people's faces, and this approach can help you go the extra mile to truly connect with your patients and loved ones.

It all starts with a Tibetan practice called nyingje, which means "king of heart," or compassion. It's more than just a feeling; it's a way of life that can transform your outlook. Think of it as the root canal of your personal growth—digging deep to remove what doesn't serve you and filling the void with kindness. Nyingje is the golden rule with a gold crown, a practice that encourages you to treat others with warmth, affection, and generosity.

Just like a good dental plan, your motivation is the "why" and the spark behind setting an intention. Motivation gets you in the door, but intention-setting is what keeps you smiling through the toughest procedures. It's about deliberately deciding to practice compassion and kindness throughout your day. For instance, before you even pick up your first tool, you could set the intention to not just fix a tooth, but to make your patient feel heard and cared for. This simple act turns a routine appointment into a moment of human connection. It's about bringing a little more floss-ophy into your daily routine.

This approach isn't just for the office; it's a practice for your personal life, too. Nyingje, with its blend of empathy and reason, helps you build deeper connections with your family and friends. It's a reminder that a simple act of kindness can fill a cavity of loneliness and bring a sense of joy and fulfillment. When you prioritize compassion, you're not just practicing dentistry—you're practicing humanity. And that's something to really sink your teeth into.

Looking to thrive and flourish in your daily life? Here are a couple of ways you can bring this practice into your life:

Morning Intention-Setting: Each morning, take a moment to reflect on your day. Set a specific intention to be present, kind, and compassionate with your patients and loved ones. You could even write it down on a sticky note and place it where you'll see it.

A "King of Hearts" moment: Throughout the day, try to find one small way to go above and beyond for a patient, a team member, or a family member. It could be as simple as an extra kind word, a genuine question about their day, or a small gesture that shows you care. This will help you keep your heart lamp aglow.

What's one small intention you can set for yourself tomorrow to make a difference in someone's day?

After 46 years in this chair, I've seen it all. I've watched technology evolve from bulky X-ray machines to 3D scanners, and I've seen the profession change in ways I never could have imagined. But I'm here to tell you that the most powerful instrument you'll ever hold isn't a high-speed drill or a state-of-the-art laser. It's something far more fundamental, and it's been the foundation of my practice for decades.

The Golden Rule with a Gold Crown

In our field, it's easy to get caught up in the technical grind—the precision of a perfect filling, the challenge of a complex extraction. But the real secret to a fulfilling career lies in what the Tibetans call nyingje, or "king of heart," which we know as compassion.

Now, don't just brush this off as a soft skill. Nyingje is the root canal of your professional life—it's about digging deep to get to the core of what truly matters. It's more than just being polite or gentle. It's a combination of empathy and reason, a blend of kindness, warmheartedness, and a genuine feeling of connection with the person in your chair. This is what separates a good practitioner from a great one. You can have all the certifications in the world, but without this, your work will always feel like a temporary fix, not a lasting bond.

Setting Your Intention

You can feel all the compassion in the world, but it doesn't mean a thing unless you put your money where your mouth is. This is where intention-setting comes in. Motivation is the spark that gets you to work, but intention is the deliberate act that makes every moment meaningful. Before you pick up that first tool, set an intention: "I will not just fix this tooth, I will make this patient feel heard and cared for."

This practice transforms your daily routine. A nervous child isn't just a patient to be sedated; that child is a small person whose fear you intend to ease. An anxious adult isn't just a number on a chart; that adult is an individual you intend to comfort and reassure. This is the simple floss-ophy that has sustained me for over four decades. It keeps the heart lamp aglow and ensures you never lose the joy in your work.

Building Bridges, Not Just Bridges

Nyingje is the easiest and best way to connect with people and build trust. When you practice this, your work becomes about more than just a dental procedure. You're building bridges—not the kind we place in the mouth, but a lasting connection with the person on the other end.

This is my legacy, and I urge you to make it yours. It's what will bring you peace, joy, and fulfillment, and it's what will make your patients come back to you year after year.

What's one small intention you will set for yourself tomorrow to make a difference in someone's day?

The career path for a dental surgeon is often seen as a straight shot to success, but even in our field, things can get a little molar-shaking. As you move from practice to partnership, or even consider a career change, you might find yourself navigating a mid-career crisis. It's a moment when the comfortable routines of drilling and filling suddenly feel like a root canal of uncertainty. This isn't a failure; it's an opportunity to re-examine your professional floss-ophy.

Lateral Moves: The Smart Extraction

When you've spent years perfecting your craft, it's easy to get tunnel vision. You see yourself as an expert in one specific area, but the truth is your skills are far more portable than you think. Trying to find another similar role in a tightening market is like trying to find a perfect fit for a mismatched crown—it's just not going to happen.

The smart move is to pivot laterally. Instead of trying to go higher within the same specialty, look for opportunities in related sectors where your expertise can shine. For instance, your skills in patient management and precision work are a perfect fit for medical device sales or product development. The way you manage a team and a multi-million-dollar practice budget is a transferable skill that could be a huge asset in healthcare administration or even in a start-up. Think of it as pulling a tooth to make room for a new, healthier one.

Clarity Is the Key to a Brighter Smile

The antidote to professional crisis is clarity. Stop seeing your career as a ladder and start viewing it as a jungle gym. It's full of sideways moves, pauses, and even backward steps that ultimately lead to a stronger position. You are not your job title. You are a leader, a meticulous problem-solver, a skilled communicator, and a manager of complex systems.

Don't be shy about getting a professional to help you articulate your story. Investing in a CV strategist isn't a sign of weakness; it's like using an intra-oral scanner for a perfect impression—it's about getting the most precise and modern representation of your skills. You need a coherent narrative that shows you're not just a dentist, but a versatile professional with a lot to offer.

You Are More Than Your Practice

Remember this single truth: "This moment, no matter how disorienting, does not define you. You have stood at crossroads before. You have taken risks, made leaps, built something from nothing. You can do it again. Reinvention is not a failure; it's an evolution."

You've built a practice from the ground up, managed a team, and brought smiles to countless faces. That resilience and skill didn't disappear with a job loss or a career hiccup. This is just a chance to apply your proven abilities in a new setting. For those willing to refocus, reframe, and realign, the odds are no longer against them, but in their favor. It's time to show the world that you've still got the professional bite you've always had.

13

THE FINAL POLISH

Looking back, it all seemed so simple. You bought a practice, you filled a schedule, you grew a reputation. The career ladder was a clear-cut path, each rung a new patient, a new procedure, a new piece of technology. I built my practice one tooth at a time, each crown, each filling, a testament to my skill and dedication. I was a craftsman, a healer, and a small business owner all in one. My life was a steady rhythm of morning coffee, a full day of drilling and billing, and the satisfied feeling of a perfect impression. I believed my professional legacy was cemented in the porcelain and composite I placed for my patients. But as I've learned, even the most perfect restoration can face unexpected trauma.

For me, the moment of crisis wasn't a sudden job loss, but a slow, persistent ache—a cracked tooth in the foundation of my professional identity. Maybe the market shifted, or a personal circumstance forced a sudden stop. The secure world I had so carefully crafted felt like it was crumbling. I found myself in a state of professional limbo, a place where all my finely honed skills—from the meticulous hand-eye coordination of a root canal to the delicate art of persuading a nervous patient—felt confined to a world that was closing its doors to me. Trying to find a new position in the same dental chair felt like a fool's errand. It was time for a new procedure.

A New Floss-ophy: The Lateral Extraction

My most important lesson was this: true reinvention isn't about looking for a new ladder to climb; it's about swinging over to a different jungle gym. My years as a private practitioner weren't just about teeth. I was a CEO, a manager, a leader, and a compassionate communicator. The skills I'd perfected in a 3x5-foot operatory were, in fact, boundless.

Think of it this way: the ability to diagnose a complex case is the same as identifying a market need. The patience required to perform a delicate endodontic procedure is the same focus needed to develop a new medical device. The empathy you show to a child in the chair is the same quality that makes for a successful patient advocate or a mentor to others. Instead of seeing my career as a straight-line story, I began to see it as a collection of portable skills. My expertise in sterilization protocols could be invaluable to a food safety startup. My years of managing a team and a budget were the very skills a healthcare consulting firm was looking for. This wasn't a downgrade; it was a lateral extraction, removing the old context to make space for a new, healthier professional life.

Reinventing the Narrative: From Dental Records to a New Resume Retired but relevant, not a fused bulb.

The hardest part was articulating this new vision. My resume was a list of dental certifications and professional associations. It didn't tell the whole story. I needed to move beyond the gilded cage of my profession and craft a new narrative. I realized that my most valuable asset wasn't my ability to use a high-speed drill, but my inherent qualities—my attention to detail, my leadership, my unwavering commitment to my patients.

I hired a professional to help me find the right language, someone who could translate my expertise from a dental chart into a dynamic resume. It was like getting a new smile design—a modern, clean, and confident look that reflected the professional I had become, not just the one I used to be. The result was a story that presented me as a versatile leader with a unique, compassionate perspective—a valuable asset in any field.

This final chapter isn't about saying goodbye to the profession I loved. It's about recognizing that the tools I mastered—the precision, the empathy, the quiet resilience—were never just for a dentist. They were for a life. My practice may have been my life's work, but my life's legacy is far greater. It's in the ability to adapt, to pivot, and to find a new way to floss-ish in a world that's always changing.

What part of your own professional journey, outside of dentistry, do you think holds the most transferable skills?

In the complex world of dentistry, we often focus on the tangible, the materials, and the mechanics. However, an emerging perspective rooted in both ancient wisdom and modern physics suggests a deeper, more profound connection between our thoughts and our professional reality. This isn't just about a positive mindset; it's about harnessing a fundamental principle of existence to elevate our practice and overcome the challenges of today.

Quantum entanglement, a concept once dismissed by Einstein as "spooky action at a distance," describes how two particles can be so intertwined that a change in one instantly affects the other, regardless of the physical distance separating them. This isn't science fiction; it's a proven aspect of reality. This principle finds a striking parallel in the ancient Advaita Vedanta philosophy, which champions the idea of "oneness in existence" — the notion that everything is interconnected within a unified field of consciousness. For the dental surgeon, this isn't an abstract concept; it's a profound lens through which to view our role.

Our thoughts, too, are a material process—a symphony of billions of neurons firing, generating electrical impulses that sculpt our reality. The wisdom of the Bhagavad Gita, as articulated by Sri Krishna powerfully states, "Thoughts become things; we become what we think." This is not a metaphor; it's a cosmic blueprint. We are the architects of our destiny, not merely by our actions, but by the very thoughts and attitudes we cultivate. The "Law of Attraction" and the "Law of Abundance" are not just spiritual clichés; they are practical applications of this universal principle. What we focus on expands. A mindset of lack and competition will inevitably attract more of the same, while a mindset of abundance and innovation will open new doors, even in a saturated market.

Today's dental landscape is a fiercely competitive arena, marked by rapid advancements in AI, robotics, and biomaterial science. While these external factors are undeniably important, the greatest leverage lies within. The principle of quantum entanglement suggests a direct link between our inner world and our outer reality. A surgeon consumed by negative thoughts, fear of competition, and a fixed mindset will find their practice mirroring this internal state—marked by stress, conflicts, and professional stagnation. "As a man thinketh in his heart, so is he."

Conversely, a dental professional who cultivates a positive, solution-oriented mindset—one that sees competition as a catalyst for growth and embraces new technologies like AI not as a threat but as a powerful ally—will find his or her practice thriving. He or she becomes a magnet for success, attracting not just patients, but opportunities, innovations, and a more fulfilling professional life. The quantum entanglement of our consciousness with our professional environment means that by refining our thoughts, we are, in essence, refining our reality.

In a world where the only constant is change, and where AI and new materials are reshaping our field at an unprecedented pace, our thoughts are our most powerful tool. "The mind is its own place, and in itself can make a heaven of hell, a hell of heaven." For the modern dental surgeon, this is not just a poetic notion; it is a practical call to action. By mastering our minds, we can master our profession and create a future of abundance, regardless of the external challenges.

Conclusion

From the Ashes, a Phoenix Rises: A Guide to Redemption

The serpent in my garden was a part of me—a shadow I nurtured in my ignorance. It was a lie I told myself, a weakness I allowed to take root. But the moment I recognized the venom, the moment I saw the true face of my own shortcomings, was the moment I found my redemption.

This is not a journey of denial, but of resurrection. For those who have stumbled and seek to rise again, these are the forgotten virtues that pave the path to becoming the phoenix you were always meant to be.

1. The Foundation of Redemption: "Know Thyself" and Value Your Inner Core.

The first step in vanquishing the serpent is to stop chasing external validation. Your past mistakes do not define your worth. The trophies you failed to win, the applause that never came—these are fleeting echoes. True worth is intrinsic; it is the unwavering ground on which you stand. When you look in the mirror and see not the sum of your errors but the light of your unblemished soul, you reclaim your power. As Ralph Waldo Emerson reminds us, "To be yourself in a world that is constantly trying to make you something else is the greatest accomplishment." Let this truth be the bedrock of your new life.

2. The First Breath of Freedom: Turn Down the Noise to Tune into Your Soul.

The cacophony of regret and the shouts of your inner critic are the loudest distractions. To find your way back, you must seek silence. In the quiet of your own mind, away from the chatter of what-ifs and the demands of others, your true voice will emerge. It is the whisper of your own wisdom, the gentle nudge of your intuition. It is here that you will find forgiveness and a new direction. As the proverb goes, "Silence is golden." It is in the stillness that your soul can sing its song of rebirth.

3. The Balm for a Wounded Spirit: Self-Love: A Daily Ritual.

You cannot heal if you are constantly at war with yourself. Loving yourself is not an act of arrogance; it is an act of survival. It is a long-term commitment to treat the person you have been, and the person you are becoming, with the same patience and kindness you would offer a cherished friend. For every mistake you've made, offer compassion. For every misstep, offer understanding. The Buddha's words ring true: "You yourself, as much as anybody in the entire universe, deserve your love and affection." Let this be the daily ritual that mends your fractured spirit.

4. The Phoenix Sheds Its Feathers: Shed the Masks, Reveal the Authentic Self.

The serpent in your garden thrived on the lies you told yourself and the masks you wore for others. To rise again, you must shed these false identities. The labels others have placed on you—failure, outcast, lost cause—are just costumes. They are not your essence. It is time to let go and break free from the shackles of what you were expected to be. This is a brave act of defiance against your past. As Shakespeare famously implored, "To thine own self be true." Only then can your authentic self emerge, whole and untainted.

5. The Alchemist of Your Destiny: Your Mind Is the Architect of Your World.

The biggest battle is not with the world, but with your own mind. The thoughts of a past full of mistakes can become a prison. But you hold the key. The thoughts you entertain are the seeds you sow for your future. To rebuild your life, you must become the master gardener of your mind, planting beliefs that empower you, not those that hold you captive. As John Milton wrote, "The mind is its own place, and in itself can make a heaven of hell, a hell of heaven." Choose to build a heaven.

6. The Currency of a New Beginning: Gratitude Is the Key to Unlocking Abundance.

Your past may feel like a barren wasteland, but there is always something to be grateful for. Counting your blessings is not just a feel-good exercise; it's a magical key that unlocks the door to a new life. A grateful heart acts as a magnet, attracting more of what it appreciates. When you are grateful for the very air you breathe, the smallest kindness, or the lesson learned from your fall, you fill your life with new light. As the old saying goes, "An attitude of gratitude is the mother of all virtues."

7. The Lionheart's Roar: Courage Is Not the Absence of Fear, but the Mastery of It.

The journey of redemption is fraught with fear—fear of failure, fear of judgment, fear of falling back into old habits. But fear is a ghost in the machine; it only has power if you give it some. Acknowledge your fears, look them in the eye, and let them know they are not the ones driving the bus. Your power is greater than their voice. As Franklin D. Roosevelt famously said, "The only thing we have to fear is fear itself." Find the courage not to be fearless, but to act in spite of it.

8. The Vessel of Your Resurrection: Honor Your Body as a Sacred Temple.

To rise like a phoenix, you must honor the vessel that carries your spirit. Your body is not a machine to be driven into the ground; it is a sacred temple. The mistakes of the past may have taken a toll, but this is your chance to repair and renew. Treat it with the respect it deserves—fuel it with nourishing foods, move it with joy, and give it the rest it needs. As the proverb states, "A healthy body is a guest-chamber for the soul." A renewed body will give you the strength to climb.

9. The Phoenix Finds Its Flock: Your Tribe Determines Your Vibe.

The isolation of your past may have made you wary of others, but no one rises alone. You are the average of the five people you spend the most time with. To redeem yourself, you must sever ties with those who enabled your past and seek a tribe that uplifts and believes in you. The company you keep can either lift you to the stars or drag you into the mud. Surround yourself with a flock that celebrates your victories and provides a shoulder to lean on during your struggles.

10. The Phoenix's Guiding Light: Your Inner Compass Is Never Lost.

When you feel lost at sea, when the path ahead seems obscured by the shadows of your past, the light within your own heart is the only lighthouse you need. Your intuition, your breath, and the steady beat of your heart are the anchors that will always lead you home. They are the constant in a world of change. Trust this inner compass. For you have seen the serpent in your garden, and you have chosen to rise. You have made mistakes, but now you have a greater purpose. You are ready to redeem, reconquer, and rise above, a phoenix reborn.

Surrender is not the loss of control.

It is your understanding that you never had control.

Shirdi Sai Baba

"Don't throw the baby out with the bathwater when confronting past blunders; let sleeping dogs lie regarding the pain, but remember the lessons so you don't go down the same rabbit hole again and stir up a hornet's nest."

My respects and gratitude

In my autobiography I have avoided taking names except a few. It is not that I do not have gratitude for them, but I did not wish to inadvertently miss anyone lest they feel let down. So, kindly accept my apologies with all the humility at my command.

Few have mentioned and amongst the other few whose names would love to mention is my staff of two decades My Man Friday, Mr. Venkatesh (fondly referred to as Venku), and my other assistants, Rashmi and Sonal who have stood by me in the ups and downs of my personal life They have been my sole strength and support for these five years and have helped in every possible way with no transactional relationship Hats off to them!

Another name I would like to mention is like my elder brother and former central minister, Mr. Anand Geete, and his P.S., Mr. Sunil Joshi. My relationship dates back to the time I started my practice in Dec. 1979, when I was introduced to him, and from then to date, he has been all along with me and has always been a well-wisher. and in his autobiography he has mentioned how we both used a stool outside my clinic and we would take turns to sit on it like musical chairs. My salute to him. Mr. Sunil Joshi and I have both been an integral part of my life and career. He even took the time off to attend my son's wedding. Such is his greatness. Adore you, sir!

I have interacted with hundreds of them and have helped them in many ways. Some of them may not remember me as they lack gratitude the less I speak of such characters, the better it is

Few more bidding good bye

We are all, in a sense, living on borrowed time. We know that death is the one appointment we all have, yet we live as if it's a "no-show" on our calendar. This blissful ignorance, however, is a serpent in the garden of our peace. It leaves us unprepared for the one event that will inevitably define the end of our story. We can't cheat death, but we can outsmart the chaos it often leaves behind.

The Unspoken Truth: A Reality Check

Many of us go through life on top of our game, feeling in complete control. We plan for careers, weddings, and retirement, but often fail to plan for the one certainty: the end. This is a classic case of putting the cart before the hearse. The real tragedy isn't death itself; it's a life well-lived followed by an ending that is messy, chaotic, and leaves those we love in disarray. Our ability to face this truth without fear, but with wisdom, is the ultimate measure of our maturity.

The Art of a Graceful Exit: Planning Without Panic

A key life lesson is understanding that while we can't control the "when," we can control the "how." This means facing the future with courage, not fear. It's about taking the reins on your final chapter.

Estate Planning Isn't Just for the Rich: The Supreme Court of India has rightly cautioned against giving away your assets prematurely. The heartbreaking stories of parents being abandoned after handing over their inheritance are a wake-up call. Don't be a cash cow that gets milked and then left to pasture. Work with a legal advisor to ensure that property and assets are transferred only after your passing. This isn't about distrust; it's about wisdom and protecting yourself.

Your Final Wishes: You can choose to have a quiet exit or a celebratory one. From dictating your last rites to setting up a foundation to feed the hungry, your legacy can be a final act of grace. Don't be afraid to voice these wishes in writing. Your living will and a health care power of attorney are crucial tools that ensure your medical decisions are in trusted hands, not left to a panicked family.

Tidying Up Your Digital and Physical Lives: In today's world, a messy house isn't the only thing we leave behind. Our digital footprint is vast. It's time to declutter your life, both literally and virtually. Start sorting through your possessions. Share passwords for your phone and online accounts with someone you trust to manage your digital afterlife. This simple act can save your family from a headache and a heartache.

The Power of Humility and Apology: Life isn't perfect, and neither are we. Part of living bravely is having the courage to apologize and seek redemption. If there are old wounds, misunderstandings, or wrongs you've committed, now is the time to make amends. A sincere apology can mend a broken relationship and bring a sense of peace that no material possession can provide. It's about facing the end with a clean slate.

The Wisdom of Retirement and Letting Go

Retirement isn't just about stopping work; it's about a new beginning. It's the time to shed the old skin and embrace a new phase. It's a dress rehearsal for letting go. When you are old or ill, you might feel vulnerable, and that's when you need to be strong from within. A brave heart isn't one without fear, but one that faces it head-on. Don't let a loved one, even if they are a family member, take control of your life or scare you. It's your time to retire from the world's fears and live with peace.

Finally, once you've faced these truths and taken control of your end, you can truly say, like Paramahansa Yogananda, "I laugh at death. I am ready anytime. Eternal life is mine,' because when you've done everything in your power to live a good life and prepare for a graceful exit, you've not just prepared to die; you've fully learned how to live.

While I was on the implant society's conference committee, a young man was inducted. Though not yet on the executive committee, this individual, Dr. Rikin Gogri, who is now the national secretary, asked some profound questions. At first, I answered him casually, not grasping the depth of his queries. It was only later, upon reflection, that I realized I had not done justice to his insightful questions. That moment was a turning point. It opened my eyes to his remarkable vision and mission, and I saw his immense potential. Throughout my autobiography, I have intentionally avoided naming individuals to keep the focus broad, but this man is a rare jewel who will always stand out in my mind. His vast knowledge and selfless dedication are qualities I hope others will not only appreciate but also emulate for the good of the association. Thanks to his unwavering commitment, our association has achieved something other specialty bodies have not: we now own our own office. Given his age and wisdom, I am confident he will become an invaluable asset that every organization would be honored to have. I am certain that readers will take a leaf out of my book on Dr. Gogri and be inspired to become better individuals themselves.

CONCLUSION

"The Serpent in the Garden. A Life Unravelled," weaving in powerful quotes and idioms in both English and Hindi, will resonate deeply with my readers:

The Enduring Bloom of Redemption

As these pages draw to a close, and my life's tapestry, with all its frayed edges and vibrant threads, lies unveiled, I am reminded of a profound truth: life is not merely a journey, but a continuous pilgrimage of the soul. We are all, in essence, "wayfarers on the path of self-discovery," each step, each stumble, a lesson etched into the very core of our being. The wisdom gleaned from the darkest nights, from moments when the garden of my existence

THE ENDURING BLOOM OF REDEMPTION

seemed overgrown with the serpent's shadows, is perhaps the most precious harvest. As the English proverb states, "Adversity introduces a man to himself," and indeed, it was in the crucible of my trials that I truly began to see.

For every pain inflicted, every wound sustained, there exists a reciprocal truth: the capacity for healing, for growth, and most profoundly, for forgiveness. It is a journey that often begins not with grand gestures, but with the quiet, courageous act of seeking pardon, both from those we may have inadvertently harmed and, perhaps most crucially, from ourselves. In Hindi, we have a beautiful saying: "क्षमा वीरस्य भूषणम्" (Forgiveness is the adornment of the brave). It is a strength, not a weakness, to acknowledge one's imperfections and to strive for reconciliation. Let us remember that "to err is human; to forgive, divine." It is in this divine act of absolution that we truly set ourselves free.

We often find ourselves trapped in the echo chambers of our own perceptions, convinced that our truth is the only truth. This can lead to a poignant blindness, preventing us from truly seeing the other's perspective. It is akin to the Hindi idiom, "अंधों में काना राजा" (Among the blind, a one-eyed man is king) – where limited vision can lead to misplaced authority and understanding. We gravitate towards those who "sing our tune," inadvertently alienating others whose narratives, though different, hold their own validity. My earnest hope is that this unraveled life serves as a humble reminder to always seek empathy, to try to "walk a mile in another's shoes," and to recognize that the human heart, in its vastness, holds room for myriad experiences and truths.

Finally, as we journey through life, relentlessly pursuing aspirations, let us pause to reflect on the true measure of our achievements. Is it the accumulation of material wealth, the "climbing of the greasy pole" through fair means or foul that ultimately defines us? Or is it the richness of our relationships, the kindness we extend, the integrity we uphold, and the quiet contentment that blossoms from a life lived with purpose and compassion? The timeless Hindi wisdom asks, **"खाली हाथ आए थे, खाली हाथ जाओगे"** (You came empty-handed, and empty-handed you shall leave). We cannot "take it with us" when our time comes to an end. Instead, let us strive to leave behind a legacy not of gold, but of genuine connection, of healing, and of love. Let our lives be a testament to the belief that the greatest wealth lies not in what we possess, but in the peace we cultivate within ourselves, and the positive impact we leave on the hearts of others.

At 63, I was on my last legs, down and out, staring into the abyss with nowhere to go. I stood at a crossroads, where one path led to the noose and the other to a desperate plea for help. I was at the end of my rope, having failed in my attempts to end my life, but I never gave up on the idea of living. I didn't beat around the bush; I reached out for a lifeline, an outstretched hand to pull me back from the brink.

I took to heart the profound words from Charlie Mackesy's book, 'The Boy, the Mole, the Fox and the Horse'. The boy asks the horse, "What's the bravest thing you've ever said?" and the horse replies, "Help," daring to show its weakness. This simple admission holds a profound truth that far too many of us are afraid to acknowledge. We let our pride get the better of us, believing we must always be the captain of our own ship, even when we're sailing into a storm.

Seeking help is not a sign of giving up; it's a courageous refusal to surrender. It's an act of faith, not in ourselves alone, but in the power of human connection. The person whose help is sought should lend a patient ear, offering not just advice but a presence. When Arjun, the mighty warrior, was torn by confusion, he didn't hesitate to seek guidance from Krishna. He knew that while knowledge is power, it's only valuable when shared.

Just as a swan glides gracefully across the water, there's a lot of paddling going on beneath the surface. We must work hard and be brave, but we must also know when to throw in the towel and ask for a lifebuoy. While we should not hesitate to seek help, it should not be our immediate response to every challenge. Don't be a crutch-walker, but also don't be afraid to ask for a helping hand when you're drowning. It's not a weakness to admit you need help; it's a testament to your strength and a refusal to give up.

May my story be a beacon, a gentle whisper of hope that even in the deepest shadows, redemption is possible, and that every wound, when tended with care, can transform into a source of profound strength and compassion. For in the grand tapestry of life, every thread, even the most tangled, contributes to a design far more intricate and beautiful than we could ever imagine. Thank you for walking this path with me.

ACKNOWLEDGMENTS

The journey of writing "The Serpent in the Garden: A Life Unraveled" has been, in itself, a profound process of reflection and growth. This book, while deeply personal, stands on the shoulders of giants – the many brilliant minds whose wisdom, articulated in their writings, has illuminated my path and shaped my understanding of life's complex tapestry.

I extend my deepest gratitude and heartfelt appreciation to the numerous authors and timeless philosophical and spiritual texts that have served as invaluable mentors. Their insights have guided me through moments of profound doubt, helped me conquer personal fears, and ultimately led me toward a more peaceful and purposeful existence.

From the ancient wisdom embedded in texts like the Bhagavad Gita and the Ramayana, which offered frameworks for understanding duty, destiny, and the human condition, to the profound teachings of spiritual leaders such as the Dalai Lama, whose emphasis on compassion and inner peace became a guiding light, their words have been a constant source of solace and direction.

Philosophers like Voltaire, Lao Tzu, and Sophocles have provided invaluable lenses through which to view the struggles with truth, doubt, and the interplay between free will and fate. Literary giants such as William Shakespeare (particularly works like The Merchant of Venice and Macbeth) and poets like Emily Dickinson have enriched my understanding of human nature, the nuances of betrayal, and the enduring power of hope.

Contemporary thinkers and business leaders like Harsh Goenka have offered practical wisdom on professional life, succession, and the art of knowing "when to hang up your drill," insights that resonated deeply with my own professional journey and transition.

While it is impossible to name every single contributor who has touched my soul with his or her profound thoughts, this entire collection of reflections, insights, and lessons is a testament to their enduring impact. Their collective wisdom forms the silent bedrock upon which my own understanding has been built, transforming personal tribulations into universal truths. All due credit is enthusiastically given to each and every one of them for helping me navigate the labyrinth of life and ultimately find my way back to light.

I am sure that my memoir, which truly sounds like a powerful contribution, and this acknowledgment will undoubtedly enhance its impact by showing the rich intellectual and spiritual tapestry that supported my incredible journey.